# DRAMA ANYTIME

Jill Charters
Anne Gately

Distributed in the U.S.A.
by
HEINEMANN EDUCATIONAL BOOKS, INC.
70 Court Street
Portsmouth, New Hampshire 03801

Primary English Teaching Association

ISBN 0 909955 64 6
Dewey 372.66
First published September 1986
Copyright © Primary English Teaching Association 1986
PO Box 167 Rozelle NSW 2039 Australia
Cover design by Mark Jackson
Photographs by Mark Norman and Christopher Simkin
Printed in Australia by
The Dominion Press-Hedges & Bell
Maryborough Vic 3465

# Foreword

| | |
|---|---|
| Scene One | An ordinary classroom; children shouting and more or less out of control, swarming all over their teacher — a lover of Shakespeare who was trying desperately to convince himself that they were being 'creative'. We knew not what we did. |
| Scene Two *(later)* | Children lying on the ground giggling and poking each other, or in listless groups making up vacuous skits . . . and always one sharp, insistent and precocious voice raised: 'Sir, why are we doing this?' In truth, we knew not why we did it. |
| Scene Three *(later still)* | Infants-in-role on a mysterious and important journey . . . until we tiptoed out of the door and the drama journey got quite forgotten amid the irrelevant delights of sunshine and traffic. My first lesson with infants: I knew what to do, and why, but not how. But we did not have this book then. I wish I had had. |

In the last two decades, drama in education has found its way. Those hopeful and often disastrous experiments need no longer happen. A clear rationale and simple practical methods have emerged to *ensure* that drama can be both valuable and successful for the ordinary teacher. Yesterday I watched a second-year student teacher, with little drama training, and a class of Grade 6 children who had done no classroom drama, exploring the Eureka Stockade through drama; at the end, they wrote miners' letters home that were longer, more careful and better than any writing their teacher and their principal had ever seen from them. The student was not exceptional; nor was her training. It was simply the *power of the medium*, simply and carefully applied. I can't wait for the next lesson . . . and nor can the children.

The possibility of this territory for learning has been opened up by leaders of vision like Dorothy Heathcote and Gavin Bolton in the U.K. (under both of whom Anne Gately has studied). In Australia, an expanding network of drama consultants, State Associations, tertiary courses and plain good teachers has surveyed and mapped the terrain. Teaching resources are now easily available, and this book is a timely addition, which by itself can provide teachers in primary schools with the basic tools to guarantee a rich harvest.

John O'Toole
*Head, Expressive Arts*
*Brisbane CAE (Mount Gravatt Campus)*

# Contents

# Introduction

You are probably already teaching drama as part of the curriculum. Role play, movement exercises and dramatised stories are probably a regular part of your class's experience. This book will assist you to find new and more varied ways of using drama, both for its own intrinsic value and as a teaching strategy throughout the whole school curriculum.

For some, however, the idea of teaching drama is overwhelming and evokes responses that suggest inexperience and lack of confidence rather than a lack of knowledge:

- —Oh, I couldn't do that! I'm not creative.
- —You've never met my class. They'd just riot.
- —I couldn't stand the noise they'd make.
- —But my kids would never want to do that.
- —That's all very well, but the children shouldn't just be having fun.
- —My Year 6 likes to get marks for things. How can I mark this?
- —The principal wouldn't let me.
- —Look, I'm flat out already. There just isn't time to fit in any drama.

These common concerns for teachers often lead them to exclude drama from their programs, and they have inspired any number of 'ideas' books. Ideas are important to you and your class in coming to an understanding about what *you* mean by drama and what *they* need in drama. But ideas alone are not enough for successful drama teaching. Planning is necessary too, and that can only be undertaken once some familiarity with basic structures has been achieved.

As with any other curriculum area, there is no one correct way to teach or to learn drama. All drama experiences can be tailored to the needs of one particular group of children—in this case, yours. This book is intended to help you find the approach that is right for your particular situation.

# 1 Why Drama?

From the very early years, parents use dramatic techniques to teach their children language. Animated faces repeat words and talk to the child about what is happening long before he or she is able to talk:

> 'And here's your beautiful red pants. Look, we'll put these on and then we'll go walking, and all the people will see you and see how beautiful you are.'

> 'Now Mummy will have some—and now you have some. Here comes the shiny shovel with all these lovely vegies, and in it goes.'

> 'This little pig went to market. This little pig stayed at home . . .'

> 'What will Mummy say when I tell her what a good boy you've been? She'll say, "Daddy, we've got the best boy in the world." '

In cold black and white some of this loving talk may look a little embarrassing. But it is part of children's early language experience and helps the child to understand the importance of language. This understanding leads to the child's striving to acquire language in order to participate in all sorts of important communications.

When we look at the way adults talk to very small children, we can see many dramatic techniques being used. For instance, the red pants are first given importance as part of the image of the child, and then there's that important leap to visualisation—'we'll go walking'—which shows that the adult is thinking about another scene and imagining what might happen. All drama is 'what might happen in these circumstances with these people at this time.'

The 'shiny shovel with the vegies' acquires a life of its own through the magic hand that guides it, just as puppets and cartoons acquire a life of their own when animated by somebody. Of course they have no real life of their own, but they do seem to have when a person takes over. Rhymes and games are equally a part of children's early language development. They teach children that learning is fun and show just how much can be learnt when people are enjoying themselves. In fact children have learnt many of their language structures by the time they come to school, and they also know a lot about basic survival, which they have learnt through their own experience.

Taking on roles and 'stepping into another person's shoes' is an important element of all drama. Role plays are often used in educational settings too as a teaching strategy. Using role play allows teachers and children to involve themselves in fictional situations and to interact with other people in role. Parents and carers take on roles all the time. Daddy may not think it's odd to pretend to be the big, bad wolf when talking to a child, and the child very readily accepts that adults often talk in role. That is why so many children's games are of the 'Now I'll be . . . and you'll be . . . and I'll come in and say . . .' variety. Children have early learnt the uses of pretending, which enables them to try out lots of different language structures and situations. They can use big, deep voices and high, quavering voices; they learn the tone of anger and the tone of persuasion.

Drama in the classroom is important in that it continues and develops this early experience, thus broadening children's understanding of language. In the primary school, language acquisition and development are two of the most important objectives for drama. They are the objectives most readily achieved and they are objectives which apply from Kindergarten to Year 6.

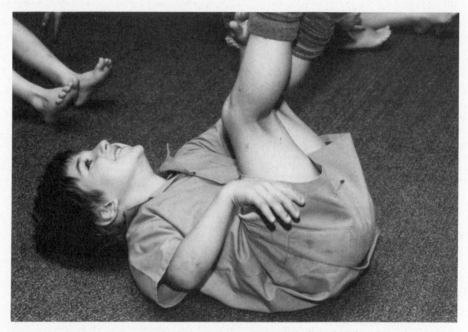

*All learning is enhanced when children are enjoying themselves.*

# *Continuation of the early years of play*

From early childhood, children enjoy and learn from play. Play is a way of representing the world which children experience, and in play they try to understand their experiences of the world around them. Socially acceptable behaviour, social interaction and many other skills are developed in play. Children learn to manipulate different sorts of objects, from balls to pegboards and puzzles. They learn about games with others, about sharing toys and spaces with other children. They become involved in co-operative ventures, such as building sand-castles and roads in sand-pits. They learn to discuss the games they are playing and to accept ideas for changing and modifying existing games. In short, they learn to get along with other people and to create new experiences with others.

# Drama as a group activity

Classroom drama is a continuation of the co-operation and collaboration of the early childhood years. Instead of competitive learning experiences, drama gives children learning experiences which depend on collaboration and co-operation. In drama, children continue to learn through being involved in imagined situations and through making decisions and interacting with others as though they were different people. They continue to use the skills they learnt in the sand-pit of creating places and situations from imagination. These skills can be developed to encompass real places and situations in order to solve real-life problems, which may occur now or later in their lives. The continuation and structuring of play into drama allows for the development of the earliest form of learning. Developing rather than diminishing this form of learning enriches education.

# Children's experiences of drama

Children's most common received experience of drama comes with watching television and film. Most pre-schoolers have some idea of drama for performance because they have watched a television program which has a story with characters who move and speak in an imaginary situation. Some children will have had experience of live theatre, especially theatre which occurs within the community in which they live. (Local festivals and concerts are quite often planned with a young audience in mind.)

Drama in school can help children to become more discriminating in their use of the media. Through being involved in their own drama experiences, they become more aware of what is being presented to them — the quality of performances, the quality of stories, the distinction between fantasy and reality. Because they too have 'made their own dramas', they begin to see how other people make drama. They are better able to choose between watching someone else's ideas come to life and making their own come alive. Whilst television watching is not an entirely passive activity (minds and imaginations are always busy), active participation in creating drama can lead to greater understanding of how the elements of drama are manipulated for the media — and how the audience is manipulated.

Children often use their media heroes and heroines as the basis for drama. This is a very good starting point, but teachers can develop from it by helping the children to see how they can go beyond stereotypes towards broader and deeper characters and situations.

# Drama in society

One of the prime uses of drama in our society is that of interpreting the culture in which we are living and looking at the cultures of other people. For a very long time, people have been using drama as a form of reflection, of celebration and of teaching. Drama is used to pass on the stories and history of cultures, and to assist young people to gain an understanding of what has gone before them and what currently influences them. Performance occurs in most cultures, providing a link with the past and a model for future creations. In our own society we expect older students to study the classic plays of the English-speaking world, notably those of Shakespeare. Such classics are seen as relevant to the present day because they examine themes and issues in life that are still current.

These issues, such as family rivalries, the quest for political power and close personal relationships, will always affect how human beings live in their societies. They also link us to other groups and cultures, and provide a reference point for examining the similarities and differences between cultures.

# Drama in the curriculum

Through the imaginative and creative assumption of roles, children and teachers can use drama as the basis for learning about and exploring many other areas of the curriculum. Some of its applications to language, social studies, science and media studies will be examined in detail in later chapters. Drama has a high value as a teaching and learning strategy which can be applied across the range of curriculum areas in the primary school.

But drama is more than a means to another end. Children in primary schools need the opportunity to see the uses of drama in practice, and to use the literature of drama in the same way as they use stories, poetry and other forms of writing in their exploration of the world they see around them. Drama absorbs children by stimulating and developing the imaginative and creative potential of each person involved.

# 2   Continuing Play

One excellent way of introducing drama to a class or group is through play activities. Many of the games that children play among themselves have a strong element of drama and some involve elaborate role playing. Group games are often highly structured with set movements, rhythmic chants and sometimes complex rules and conventions. For example, anyone who watches some of the skipping and other group games in progress in the playground will be struck by the children's display of coordination, rhythm and sheer discipline, as well as by the exuberant enthusiasm being generated. Creativity will be evident as children improvise on well-established forms to produce ingenious variations and imaginative transformations of standard games. Note how games are modified to suit groups of different sizes and varying ages. Any school playground will provide you with a wealth of examples of children happily engaged in activities in which there is a spontaneous but disciplined merging of physical, vocal and creative elements.

For many teachers harnessing the creative energy of the playground and adapting and moulding it to suit the classroom will be the most natural way to introduce drama. Bringing games into the classroom gives you a ready-made vehicle for establishing cooperative group spirit and for creating the atmosphere in which further drama activities can grow. Whereas in the playground children will usually play in 'set' groups, often confined to members of one sex, in the classroom they can be encouraged to become involved in games that involve more fluid groupings including both sexes. In this way individual children can broaden their range of social contacts, and a more diverse mix of social interaction will evolve naturally.

This chapter presents a store of ideas for drama games. All of them can be adapted to suit different age groups and different levels of physical and intellectual development. The selection is by no means exhaustive, and you will be able to add your own variations and develop new ideas.

## Some points to consider

In choosing drama games for use with a particular class you should be aware of any individuals within the class who may have difficulty in taking part. For instance, some children, especially younger ones, are unable to accept any form of 'missing out' or losing and become distressed when they are out of a game. There may be others who naturally shun the limelight and try to avoid being chosen for a conspicuous role in any game. You should be conscious of these potential problems and treat these feelings as sympathetically as possible, whilst encouraging reluctant children to participate in all facets of the games. They will probably be able to overcome their inhibitions more easily in the context of a game than in what they perceive as a more formal drama situation.

Although games that involve vigorous movement can usually be adapted for indoor use, there will always be some children who find it more difficult than others to rein in their natural exuberance and restrict their movements for smaller spaces. For this reason you may choose to begin with games that require little or only gentle movement, and progress to games that involve rapid movement only when the children become more accustomed to using the available space.

Again, you may prefer to begin with some of the games and exercises for small groups. Several groups can play different games simultaneously, or one group at a time can be involved in a game while the rest of the class does other things.

*Drama allows for diversity in learning and social interactions.*

# The teacher's role

In all these activities you should exercise a firm but unobtrusive control, watching the interactions of children within groups. Be aware of children who may try to dominate and offer them alternatives, such as being the leader in the next game. Support children who feel shy about taking part by taking part yourself with them.

It's also likely that in playing games over a period some children will display strengths — such as leadership potential or qualities of imagination and creativity — which can be used to advantage in other drama activities.

In some games you will no doubt wish to take an active part while structuring the proceedings. In others, depending on the game and the nature of the group, you may decide to supervise from the outside. In general, the more you play with your children, the greater the rapport you are likely to establish with your class, and the better prepared the children will be to accept you as a role player in other drama activities.

# Sitting circle games

## Fruit bowl
All the players sit on chairs in a large circle, except one who is the caller for the game. You can either join the seated group or become the first caller.

The caller numbers each of the sitting players 'one' or 'two'. When the group has been numbered, all the 'ones' become bananas and all the 'twos' become pineapples. The caller then takes up a position in the centre of the circle and calls out one of the following instructions:
   — 'Bananas!' This means that all bananas must change seats.
   — 'Pineapples!' This means that all pineapples must change seats.
   — 'Fruit bowl!' Everyone must change seats.
When 'fruit bowl' is called, the caller also has a chance to grab a seat. The player left standing becomes the new caller, and the previous caller assumes the identity (banana or pineapple) of the player who has become the new caller.

This game can be varied by changing the names into those of animals (thus making a game of 'zoo') or plants (making a game of 'garden'). You can encourage your children to change the fruits, animals or plants, so that a wider vocabulary can be explored.

## Do you like your neighbours?
As in 'fruit bowl', the players sit in a circle and the caller stands in the middle. The caller asks any child in the circle, 'Do you like your neighbours?' If the answer is 'Yes', the two people sitting on either side of him or her must swap chairs while the caller makes a bid to grab one of the chairs. If the answer is 'No', everyone must change chairs and the caller also tries to grab a chair. The player left without a chair becomes the new caller.

## Everyone who . . .
This game calls for imagination and quick thinking, and some children may need help until they get used to it.

The group sits in a large circle with a caller in the centre. (Until the class has some experience of the game, it's probably best for you to act as first caller.) The caller calls out a description beginning with the words 'Everyone who' — for example:
   Everyone who caught a bus to school.
   Everyone who is wearing sneakers.
   Everyone who has blue eyes.
Every player for whom the description is true must change chairs with another who is at least three places away in the circle. (This number can be reduced if the game is being played with a small group.) The player left without a seat becomes

the new caller and the game continues. No description may be repeated in the same game.

To help children who have trouble thinking up descriptions, you might suggest particular categories — e.g., clothes, tastes in music or television programs, food eaten for breakfast.

# Cooperative exercises

## Proo

Each child stands in his or her personal space in the classroom. (The idea of personal space is explored in Chapter 4.) You begin by asking everyone to stand still and quiet, with eyes closed, and then set the scene with a description like this:

> You have just landed, alone, on an alien planet and you are experiencing a very strange sensation: you can't see anything around you, but you're aware that there are other beings near you. As you walk carefully about this planet, you occasionally bump into some of these beings, and they shake hands with you and say 'Proo'. This seems to be the only word they use and it's a form of greeting.

You then allow some time for the children to move about the classroom, greeting each other as described. Children who have trouble keeping their eyes shut or who become nervous gigglers will need some special help. When the children are moving quietly around the room, except for occasional greetings of 'Proo', you can go on:

> As you move about you are aware that these beings are friendly, but you discover, by accident, that there is an alien in your midst. [At this point you nominate an alien by tapping one child on the shoulder.] None of you knows who it is, but it has the effect of changing the atmosphere of friendliness. If you meet up with the alien you will know, because it shakes hands but doesn't say 'Proo'. When this happens you remain linked to the alien by the hand and must move about with it. If others bump into you they recognise that you too have become an alien, because you no longer say 'Proo', and they must stay attached to you.

As the game proceeds, there is an ever-growing clump of silent people moving about the room, trying to ensnare the friendly beings who still say 'Proo'. Children quickly learn that the game is much more enjoyable if everyone plays by the rules; if anyone other than the nominated alien remains silent, or if players cheat by opening their eyes, the game is over far too quickly. You might help set the atmosphere by providing blindfolds for the whole group.

## Lighthouse and rocks

The children sit on the floor in their own personal space, making sure that there is enough room for someone to walk right around them without treading on fingers or bumping into a neighbour. One child is chosen for the ship. The ship is blindfolded and led to a corner of the room. You then silently nominate another child as the lighthouse. The lighthouse goes to the corner diagonally opposite the ship. All the other players are rocks.

The ship must move diagonally across the room, guided by the lighthouse which is making 'beep-beep' sounds. When the ship comes close to a rock, the rock makes a swishing noise to imitate waves splashing against rocks. If the ship goes aground by bumping into a rock, a new ship is chosen and the game starts again. The lighthouse, too, should be changed from time to time.

## Human snake

The children stand in a long straight line (it may curve if the room is too small). Each player faces the back of the player in front. The front player reaches back with the right hand between his or her legs and grasps the left hand of the player behind. The second player and then each of the others in turn does the same, until the whole line is joined together. Then, beginning with the last player in the line, the whole 'snake' gradually lies down. If this is managed without the line breaking up, the snake tries to stand up again.

This game is useful for developing controlled movement as well as group cooperation. It's an enjoyable short 'fill-in' activity.

## Shopping list

You sit in a circle with the children and begin by saying, 'I went shopping and I bought some tomatoes.' The next person adds to the list: 'I went shopping and I bought some tomatoes and a lettuce.' The game proceeds with each player in turn adding a new item to the ever-growing list.

This is a good vocabulary exercise for all children, and can be made more difficult for older children by making the shopping tasks less familiar — e.g., by choosing hardware, gardening, boating or sewing items.

The game can also be varied by nominating a list of items taken on a holiday, and the degree of difficulty can be altered by choosing different kinds of holidays — e.g., at the beach, camping and bushwalking, in Central Australia, in a large city. You might use the lists as the starting point for a unit on writing or as part of a social studies unit.

## My song

The children are divided into two groups of equal numbers. Each group chooses a song that is known to all the children, and both groups simultaneously begin to sing their songs. Each group tries to win members of the other group over to its song. If a child begins to sing either the tune or the words of the other group's song, he or she must join the other group and continue to sing its song. The game finishes when everyone is singing the same song.

With new players of any age it's a good idea to begin with nursery rhymes, such as 'Baa Baa Black Sheep' or 'Mary had a Little Lamb'. Nursery rhymes have a strong beat, and the words will probably be familiar to most children.

This game can, of course, become very noisy and needs a firm commitment from everyone to be reasonable about noise levels. One way to reduce noise and make the experience more infectiously enjoyable is to form the groups into two concentric circles. When the singing begins, the outer group walks around the room in a clockwise direction and the inner circle moves in an anti-clockwise direction.

The game can easily be integrated into a music or movement program.

## Trains and stations

One member of the class is nominated as 'train spotter' and leaves the room, while you and the other children sit in a circle with everyone holding hands. (If chairs are being used, they must be very close together.) Two or more children are designated as stations. By pressing hands around the circle, the players can send a train in one direction around the circle. When the train comes to a station, the station can either send it on in the same direction or make it change direction. Stations must indicate that the train is passing through by calling out 'Toot-toot'. When the group understands the procedure and the train is moving around the circle, the train spotter is invited back into the room and asked to pinpoint the location of the train.

In order to maintain the children's interest in the game and to give as many as possible the chance to test their powers of observation, a time limit can be set or each spotter can be limited to three guesses.

# Running games

With most running games it is important that everyone understands the rules clearly. All of the following running games can be played for their own sake, or used as physical warm-ups and energisers for other drama activities. They can also create an enjoyable break when the children are changing focus during the day from one curriculum area to another. Of course the amount of noise that some of these games inevitably generate may place some limits on the times when you can use them in a classroom.

## Crazy relays

The class is divided into two relay teams and a 'crazy' idea is chosen for a relay race. Some examples are:
- walking backwards
- walking forwards on the knees
- walking blindfolded (quiet is important here so that players can tell when they are nearing the other end of the room)
- three-legged relays
- slow motion.

## Rats and rabbits

Two walls or two objects such as desks are designated as 'rats' and 'rabbits' and a caller is appointed—at first yourself. When you call out 'Rats', everyone must go and touch the place or object that has been named 'rats', and when you call 'Rabbits', they must go and touch whatever has been named 'rabbits'. You can make false calls by calling out 'Rivers', 'Riders' and other words beginning with 'r'. Anyone who moves to the wrong place or who moves on a false call is out of the game; the last one in is the winner. The game can be varied by using other words that begin with strong consonants, such as 'boats' and 'banks', 'cars' and 'caravans', or 'trees' and 'trailers'.

Arguments can arise in this game and it's better for you to act as caller to begin with, so that there can be quick and decisive arbitration about who is in and who is out. As children become more experienced, they will be able to call.

## Streets and alleys

Two children are chosen to become a cat and a mouse and another player—yourself at first—is appointed caller. The rest of the players stand in even rows to form a square or rectangle, e.g., six rows of five children each. When they are facing one of the walls they are said to form streets, and when they turn at an angle of 45 degrees they are said to form alleys. When the caller calls 'Streets', all the players in rows face in the agreed direction and join hands. When 'Alleys' is called, they turn and join hands to become alleys. The cat tries to catch the mouse by chasing it through the constantly changing streets and alleys.

The game calls for coordinated movements and quick reactions and is probably more suitable for older children. For the first few games, until the class becomes adept at making the necessary rapid changes, it is advisable for you to act as caller.

## Caught in the middle

The class is divided into groups of three players and a caller is appointed. Two of the players in each group join hands to form a cage in which the third member of the group is caught. When the caller calls 'Break!', the players who are forming the cage break their hands apart and release the player trapped inside. The cage must then be re-formed by the same two players with a new person caught in the middle. The caller can be trapped inside a cage, and the player who is left free when all the cages have been re-formed is the new caller.

The pairs who make up the cages can be changed around during the game and can change places with the players who have to be caught.

# *Tag games*

The following variations on the familiar, traditional games of tag or chasings are a useful means of fostering group cohesion. They can also be used as physical warm-ups for other drama activities. Most of these games can be played inside, but they require large uncluttered spaces, such as empty classrooms, halls or canteen areas.

## Touch tag

A clearly defined space — e.g., from the bubblers to the far wall, or the whole hall except the stage — is designated as the area for the game, and two children are chosen as taggers. When a child is tagged, he or she replaces one of the original taggers and must hold on to the spot that was touched until he or she manages to tag another player. At any one time, then, there will be two people running around holding an elbow, knee, shoulder, back, etc.

## Sticky tag

If this game is to continue for any length of time, you will need to have plenty of sticky tape on hand.

Stick a piece of tape on the arm, elbow or shoulder of one player, who then becomes the tagger. (With a larger group the game will be more exciting if there are two or three taggers.) The tagger must try to catch another player and transfer the tape to this player without using a hand. After several such transfers the tape will lose its stickiness, and the game will proceed more smoothly if you act as supervisor and dispenser of new tape.

## Caterpillar tag

One player is chosen as tagger. When a player is tagged, he or she holds the waist of the original tagger, and as more players are tagged a giant 'caterpillar' is gradually formed. The caterpillar must be intact when anyone is being tagged. The group will quickly realise that the caterpillar's long tail can be brought around to encircle a player, who can then be tagged by the tagger at the head. The last player to be tagged is the winner.

You can join in a game of caterpillar tag and supervise quite easily from a position along the caterpillar.

### Stuck in the mud

Two or three children are chosen as taggers and made easily identifiable, e.g., by a crepe-paper ribbon, a netball vest or a softball mitt. When a player is tagged, he or she is 'stuck in the mud' and must stand still until rescued. Rescuing takes place when another player crawls between the legs of one of mud-bound players. Rescuers must try to free other players without themselves being tagged in the process.

### Hug tag

The players make a large circle and one, the tagger, stands in the centre. The tagger counts to ten and can then tag anyone who is not hugging someone else. The person who is tagged then becomes the tagger.

As this game requires an even number of players you may have to join in. Once the basic rules are understood you can add an extra dimension by ruling that players cannot hug the same person twice, or that each player must move at least two places round the circle before hugging another.

Other variations of tag include crawling tag, hopping tag, pair tag, slow-motion tag, walking tag, backwards tag, silent tag and blindfolded tag.

## Small group games and exercises

The following games and exercises can all be carried out in small groups of between four and seven people. In some of the activities a number of groups will simultaneously carry out the same task, while in others every group will be expected to make its own unique response to a particular idea.

### Trust circle

Each group stands in a circle with one member of the group in the centre. There should be some distance between each group. Each circle should be small and very stable, and each child's shoulders should be touching the shoulders of the children on either side. With eyes closed, the person in the centre allows his or her body to fall gently backwards. The others provide support by holding their hands with flat palms outwards at chest level. The person in the centre can then rock gently backwards and forwards, completely trusting the group to give support.

When children become more confident about trusting each other, the person in the centre can be passed around the circle from one member of the group to another. The circle can also be widened so that the angle and distance of the fall becomes greater. Every member should have the opportunity to be the one supported in the centre.

This activity assumes a certain level of maturity and experience and is probably not suitable for children under about nine years, or for groups that have had very little experience of drama.

## Machines

This activity can be approached in two ways:

1. In the first approach you describe a machine to the class and each group devises the action and sound for that machine. Make sure your description is pitched at a level appropriate to the children's age and previous experience. Children who have had little or no practice at role playing might be asked to simulate the relatively simple sounds and actions of machines like egg beaters, bicycles, fans, jackhammers, cranes and lawnmowers. Those with more highly developed skills could be asked to suggest the workings of robots, conveyor belts, railway signals, chain saws and butter churns, while more expert groups might be set to work at helicopters, looms, printing presses, vacuum cleaners, radio satellites, railway signal boxes and grain loaders.

Imaginary wonders such as homework doers, sunshine makers and rain scatterers can also be used to test the imagination of the more able and experienced children.

2. The second approach allows greater scope for invention. Each group is asked to construct a machine, piece by piece, and then determine its use. A group can begin with one movement and add more and more movements, until every group member has contributed something to the whole machine. Sound effects can be added to give the onlooker further clues about the uses and capabilities of the machine. Each machine can then be put through its paces by being speeded up, slowed down or taken quickly from complete standstill to high speed.

## Statues

The class is divided into groups and a 'sculptor' is appointed for each group. The sculptor's job is to shape the other members of the group into statues. These statues can tell stories, represent themes or be starting points for more complex improvisation and play building.

*The children's favourite stories can be starting points for improvisation.*

Ideas for statues that tell stories need to be geared to the age and experience of the group. Some suggestions for children who are relative newcomers to this kind of activity are:

- how the kangaroo got its tail
- the day I started school
- learning to swim
- learning to walk
- catching a crocodile
- caught in the rain
- when I got lost
- some stories from nursery rhymes (e.g., 'Little Miss Muffett'), fairy tales (e.g., *The Three Billy Goats Gruff*) or children's books (e.g., *Mr Archimedes' Bath*).

Children with more experience and maturity could construct statues to tell about:

- winning the race
- Christmas morning
- landing on the moon
- the potion that makes things invisible
- the day I was rescued
- skydiving
- stories from such books as *Kidnapped* or *Possum Magic*.

Groups with a more extensive background in drama could try their hand at statues that depict:

- the new teacher arriving
- waking up in the land of my dreams
- learning to ride a bike
- lost in the bush
- my favourite pastime
- the mutiny on the *Bounty*
- meeting my idol.

Themes can usually be adapted to different levels. When choosing themes around which to build statues you should take account of what is likely to interest the class. Some possible themes are:

- sport
- travelling
- music
- winning
- losing
- families
- adventure
- discovery
- weather
- friendship
- authority
- city life
- country life
- communication
- time machines
- accidents
- school
- media heroes

Statues can also be the starting point for improvised scenes or for building group plays, especially with students who have had a lot of experience of drama. The statues can be created as still pictures from which scenes begin, or as the points at which scenes end. In the first instance the statues come to life and continue the scenes. In the second, the group must work out in action how they came to be frozen into the positions in which they find themselves.

## Freeze frames

This activity is an extension of 'statues'. In groups the children decide on sequences of scenes, which they then present as 'freeze frames' or photographs. The number of frames a group uses to relate an incident will depend on the amount of detail the group wishes or is able to depict. Generally speaking, the more frames a group uses, the greater will be its opportunity to develop ideas and explore its subject in depth.

When a group presents a series of frames, it should be gathered at one end of the room, while the rest of the class sits facing it with eyes closed. When the first frame has been set up, a member of the group who has been appointed caller calls out 'Open', and the audience open their eyes. After about fifteen seconds the caller says 'Close', and the audience close their eyes while the second frame is set up. This procedure continues until all the frames have been viewed, and the incident or story has been completed. If the members of the audience have entered properly into the spirit of the exercise, and have remained silent and followed instructions, they will have experienced a sensation like watching a videotape being wound 'fast-forward' and stopped every so often.

This activity provides valuable training in decision-making and self-discipline. Because the frames only work when everyone in a group works closely together, it develops an understanding of the need for strict coordination and control.

The games in this chapter can prepare children for other and more extensive drama activity. What began as a warm-up exercise may develop into something capable of considerable extension and elaboration. You should be constantly aware of this possibility, and drama programs should always be flexible enough to cater for this kind of unscheduled variation.

# 3　Some Beginnings

If drama is an essential experience for children, what can it do for their teachers? How can teaching drama help the teacher? That is, how can drama help you in your teaching program and what positive contributions to your work can you look for?

Because all work in drama is, by its very nature, a co-operative venture, drama complements other forms of group work. It allows children from different friendship groups, and others who might not usually work together, in reading, writing or other curriculum areas, to find something exciting to do co-operatively. It's also an excellent way of helping girls and boys to work together without sex-role stereotyping. In drama, those with poor language skills are able to participate fully because it does not rely solely on skills in speaking, reading or writing. Ideas can be shared in movement and action. In fact, all children have a contribution to make in drama and drama allows all children to contribute. Through drama you can find a way to bring the whole group together in a collaborative, creative way.

In most classes children will have a variety of competencies in speaking, writing, reading and moving. Drama can be planned to extend those who are more competent in self-expression or in developing roles, as well to help those who are less competent in self-expression or in taking on a role and interacting with others in role. Activities can be chosen to help children who, for example, are unable to speak confidently to larger groups of their peers or to adults. Drama can develop competence in listening and moving for most children, whether as part of their improvisations or in discrete movement lessons.

Integrated programs can be built around drama. Writing and drawing can lead to and stem from drama; music is a natural partner in drama; mathematics can be part of the research work in play building and is part of movement work in drama; reading provides a wealth of ideas and sources for drama, and all language can be linked to drama. Using drama to integrate your total teaching program will enrich the program, save time and effort, and establish independent learning habits and good working relationships between children. All this does not happen in the space of a week, of course! But over a year of planned drama experiences, you would expect a class — and you, their teacher — to move through various levels of dramatic experience. Over the six or seven years of primary schooling, children will develop their skills in drama and their understandings about drama. By the time they have completed primary school, *all* children should be among those who have had lots of experience in drama.

# Levels of experience

Basically, the levels of children's dramatic experience you may expect to see in primary school can be identified as follows:

- Level 1—children with no experience
- Level 2—children with some experience
- Level 3—children with lots of experience.

Children with no experience in drama may be hesitant about taking an active or obvious part in any drama activity. They may be unable to follow through or develop ideas alone, but may be more confident in doing so in groups or when directed by another. They may rely on stereotypical characters and solutions in their drama work. Some may be unable to sustain their belief or interest in drama for long periods, but may enjoy short activities which seem to be games. None the less, these children will enjoy the experience of sustained drama as they develop other competencies, such as writing and reading, which require sustained concentration. Children who are beginning drama will rely heavily on the ideas the teacher provides for the class. You will need to plan structured lessons, with a number of different types of activities which support the children in the early stages of their development in drama.

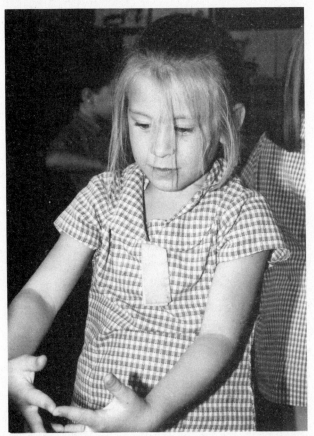

*Sustained interest in drama develops with experience.*

Children with some experience in drama will suggest topics or ideas they would like to cover. They might want to use a story or a television program that they know well as the basis for their work. They may choose to extend familiar characters and roles, such as television characters or members of their family or school community, and give them added dimension, often a humorous one. They will be better able to sustain their interest in drama activities and to collaborate well with most members of the class. There will be less desire to work only with friends or known partners.

Children with lots of experience in drama will be able to develop different roles and to choose a variety of roles. They will be able to work with most of their class-mates and will be happy to participate in drama activities with a number of different people. They will be able to sustain their interest in role plays and pick up the drama, in role, from one lesson to the next. Experienced children will be adventurous in their movement work, confident in speaking and courteous about listening. They will be able to suggest alternative structures for their drama lessons, as they will have experienced different forms of drama, and may request some of their favourite activities from time to time. Because they will be confident about exploring ideas in drama, they will want to suggest ways of using drama in many areas of the curriculum. Questions such as, 'Can we do a drama about whales/explorers/the swimming carnival/a rock band?' will become a storehouse of ideas for programming drama lessons.

# Planning the program

Drama for you and your class must take into account your interests and their needs, as well as such factors as the space you have available, the degree of skill the class already has, and the drama approach you are most comfortable with. Decide on an approach that you think will work for you first, and use the ideas in this book as a beginning. You'll find that new ideas and a more expanded range of approaches will follow.

Some factors you should consider when planning your drama program are:

### your own drama teaching skills and confidence
If you don't feel very confident about teaching drama, choose some drama activities that are very structured or very brief. Plan to do drama once a week or once a fortnight to begin with, until you feel your repertoire of skills is expanding and your confidence about teaching drama is growing.

### the time you have available for drama
The expanding curriculum in the primary years often makes teachers feel that they cannot fit another curriculum area into teaching programs. Look at ways of integrating drama as a teaching strategy within an existing program, or ways of using drama as the starting point for a unit of work in a language program.

### resources available in the school
Another member of staff may be able to provide you with ideas for programming drama, or you may be able to enlist the help of a specialist teacher or resource teacher in a drama program. Many colleagues may have books or notes from in-service courses or other courses of study which they can share with you.

### resources available outside the school
In some areas, drama consultants may be available to work with you in planning

your program and demonstrating teaching practices. Team teaching with a consultant may provide a stimulating learning experience for the class and for the teacher. Libraries may have collections of drama materials, including teacher reference books, which you can borrow. A reference list of some helpful titles is included at the end of this book.

In-service courses may be available locally or at some central location. Look out for notices of courses. Professional teacher associations for drama teachers exist in every State. Write to the National Association for Drama in Education (NADIE) for the contact in your State:

National Association for Drama in Education,
P.O. Box 168,
Carlton North, Vic. 3054

## *Starting points for drama*

There are many successful teaching strategies available as models when you begin to teach drama. You will be able to find books, videos and films which show you how a number of teachers use a number of strategies, and Chapter 8 has case studies to illustrate some. Among these strategies you will see teachers who use roles with their classes. That is, the teacher becomes a character for the class, and the class uses information or ideas gained from meeting this character. A teacher in role can give the class information which might otherwise be difficult to obtain. A meeting with Caroline Chisholm will give children more direct information about life for families in early Australia than they would be able to glean in the same amount of time spent reading about it. Similarly, meeting with an experienced trapeze artist can give children some ideas about life behind the scenes in a circus and help them to develop their own ideas about circuses.

Using a variety of starting points, including that of taking on a role yourself, you are able to contribute to the children's experience of drama. Some of these starting points are:
- using writing as the stimulus for drama, including diaries, letters, messages, accounts and pieces of dialogue
- using objects, such as household implements, tools, artefacts, pieces of clothing, paintings and pictures, which can assist the class to see what some of the characters in a drama might be like
- using a known story and developing the characters and situations from that.

## *Drama as short activities*

Short drama activities may be the most comfortable beginning for teachers with a new class, or if they themselves are new to drama. You might be just beginning to teach drama yourself and prefer a very structured activity to begin with, so that you are able to observe the class and see how they take to a co-operative, creative activity. You might use drama exercises, such as those where partners mirror each other's action, those where groups build statues depicting scenes or stories, or vocal exercises where the class can throw sounds around a circle. Exercises like these can be a very good beginning for both class and teacher as they take little preparation, are finite, clear and repetitive, and are generally within the capabilities of all the children in the class.

Keep in mind, however, that these short activities are only a beginning stage, and that groups should be able to move on to other, more exciting projects as well as taking part in exercises. Drama really takes place when we change places with someone else and step into the shoes of another character. Exercises are like practising the strokes but never actually getting down to the writing.

# Drama as a whole group activity

You might begin with a drama which involves the whole class. Whole group work takes some planning and preparation, which includes the class doing some research. For instance, if the drama is to be about reaching compromises and getting along together, then the class might be divided into two tribes who have to determine their use of common resources, e.g., water. The children might need to do some research about uses people have for water. You might need to set up a situation for them using a map: for example, 'All the water holes are here in this part of the land. How will the people over here be able to reach the water? Will we let them build a road?'

The best kind of drama with whole groups is based on dramatic role play. The role play can be extended so that participants have to develop their roles and come to some understanding of the issues they face. This is essential to any development in drama, as it relies on the participants entering into the situation and believing in it. Then a real shift in understanding takes place and the children have gained an insight into the lives of others. In *Towards a Theory of Drama in Education* (Longman, Harlow, 1979), Gavin Bolton calls this type of extended role play 'drama for understanding'.

*Belief in a role can lead to greater insight into other people's lives.*

This teaching approach to drama is particularly valuable as it enables you to plan for drama linked to other areas of the curriculum. You can use a whole group drama to teach a class concepts or skills in language, social studies, music or some area of their social development. The class also gains experience in using role, in improvising, and in shaping a drama so that it has tension and form. Children learn to work together and to use the ideas of many people to create their drama.

A good way of entering into a whole group drama is to build up the framework by finding some answers to these questions:

**Who** are we?
**Where** are we?
**When** is this action taking place?
**Why** is this happening?
**How** will we begin the story of what is happening?

Once you have established this framework, choose a point to begin the action. Some good beginning points are:

**moments of realisation**
—when we first see the smoke across the mountains
—when we know that the storm is coming
—when we notice that all the cows have stopped giving milk
—when we arrive at work to find a new boss

**the start of journeys**
—when we are choosing the cabins we want for the trip
—when we are packing our bags before boarding the space-craft
—when we have just got off the bus at the start of the dirt road

**drawing a plan of the location**
—this is what is on the island
—these are the tunnels through the mountains
—the city is laid out like this
—there are lots of rooms in this house and it's three storeys high
—the secret chamber in the museum is in the basement, but this is what the rest looks like

**reading a letter or message**
—this is what's in his will
—these are the designs of the chairs
—this message was received last night but some of it is in code
—these letters were found in a drawer under the desk

**looking at someone's belongings**
—these clothes were the ones she was wearing when they last saw her
—this umbrella and suitcase belonged to the journalist who has disappeared
—he never went into the bush without this camping gear.

All of these starting points can lead the class to achieve the objectives you have planned for the drama they are beginning. To develop the drama further, keep in mind the framework that you decided on earlier and maintain it. You can't know beforehand how things will turn out, but you can always rely on what you all agreed was to be the framework. You may end up never finding what's in the secret chamber in the museum, but you may learn a lot about what museums are for, how artefacts are cared for and why security is important.

# Drama as a small group activity

Using small groups or pairs in drama can be useful if you feel that children within one class are at different levels of dramatic experience. You might have a class which has some beginners and other children with some experience. Small groups and pairs will allow the children to work at a level most suited to their needs and interests. Because they will be working in the same space and they will be aware of the work going on around them, it's not long before the beginners see and hear how they might develop their own work. Drama in small groups or pairs allows for all children to be working simultaneously. It also allows for more than one structure — pairs can explore what has been discussed in a larger group; scenes can change because one small group might have a different ending to another.

Children can work in small groups within a whole-group drama; e.g., all the scientists might work together, while all the engineers work in a different group and all the medical staff in another. Sometimes this is more manageable, as it helps children work together without needing a lot of 'teacher input' to build their own belief in what they are doing.

Another way of using small groups is to get the class to improvise scenes or devise small plays which they might later show each other. Alternatively they might tell each other what happened in their scene. If this approach is the one you choose, make sure that the children have a real purpose in their performance. Just it 'being your turn' is not enough. Some groups may not be ready to perform and should not be forced to do so. Approaching drama in this way can be by:

- deciding on a story and having each group improvise a scene from it
  e.g., the scenes in *Mr Archimedes' Bath*
- deciding on a story and having each group make up a new ending
  e.g., what would have happened if Ned Kelly had escaped at Glenrowan?
- giving the children some roles and having them devise a scene for the roles
  e.g., a grandfather, a father, a mother, an aunt, a teenage son, a ten-year-old daughter
- giving the children a situation and having them decide what might happen
  e.g., waiting at the bus-stop in the rain
- giving each group an object to build a scene around
  e.g., a tennis racquet, a car-jack, a frying pan
- giving each group a first or last line of dialogue to begin their scene
  e.g., 'Where have you come from?'
  'That's the last time I'll try to help him!'

As with all small group work, drama in small groups requires the participants to help each other find and sort out ideas. Each individual contributes to the work of the group. This means that you might have to take some steps to make sure everyone is included in a group, or that those who might be disturbing or disrupting a group are given some help to see how they might best contribute.

# Drama as an individual activity

Many teachers feel more comfortable with drama that begins with individual activities. This approach is particularly suited to movement work. You will find that you can ask the whole class to do some movement exercises or to respond to music as individuals—either as the start of a longer lesson which goes on to small group work, or as a shorter lesson which concentrates only on developing skills. With individual activities, make sure that you have provided a space big enough for all children to participate in their own personal space. This ensures that people don't bump into each other—accidentally or on purpose. Distraction in individual activities can lead to the whole lesson breaking down, but this can be usually avoided by making sure that there's plenty of space (such as in a double classroom or hall), that it's a good time for the class (you'll know when they are at their best and worst), and that everyone knows what the sequence for the activity is. Ideas for structuring this sort of activity are detailed in Chapter 4.

## Using teacher in role

Drama allows you to widen the context of classroom language by bringing in an outside context, either real or imaginary. These outside contexts can incorporate a role for you within the drama. By working in role with the children, you will have greater scope for different teaching styles and different teaching objectives. As well as your everyday self, you can be

- a special messenger
- someone who has lost a treasure and needs help
- a visitor from far away who is bringing good news
- someone who can lead others to a new world

and a host of other characters who will be pivotal in classroom drama. Through

*Role allows teachers to be some exciting new presence in the class—and a new learner.*

your participation in role in the drama the children are doing, you will be able to be an active participant in their learning while structuring it and providing important stimulus for their further work.

There are several types of role which are suitable for teachers to use in order to assist children to develop their own ideas and explore possibilities for their own roles. Suitable roles to adopt include:

- a person who doesn't know what is happening and needs to find out
- a person who knows about dangers or conditions ahead
- a person who is second in charge (Avoid being the boss, the captain or the leader of any group. These roles are better given to children.)
- a person who needs to be looked after, because of age, infirmity, ignorance or fear
- a person who holds secret knowledge
- an historical character
- a character from fiction.

The use of role can range between giving only some slight indication of the attitudes which are held by a particular character, to using a great deal of detail so that a full picture of the role is built up. Roles for the teacher can be used in a variety of ways:

**to present information**
'I've been given this message by the guard at the gate who told me you'd all better read it and take notice of what it says.'

'There was this map pinned to the door when I came in, but I can't make much sense of it. I wondered whether someone else might know how to read maps.'

'I don't know about you but I was told that I wasn't allowed to bring any books when I came here.'

Information like this can give the group a chance to discuss possible action and development. What does the map say? How important is it that the map be kept safe? Why were we told not to bring books? Has anyone tried to smuggle in a book? What do you do when there are no books?

**to ask for information**
'I've come here to find my shadow and I don't know where to start looking.'

'How long do we have to stay in this boat?'

'Is there any one in charge here? I want to go home and I haven't got any money.'

Faced with such problems, a group of children needs to find solutions and to respond to the genuine request of a character who needs information to go on or survive.

**to question the validity of decisions**
'I don't think the boss will like it when I tell him that you don't want to go down the mine again. There are quotas we have to fill, you know.'

'If we keep going west, I think we'll get further and further away from the sea. Have we got enough supplies to go right into the centre?'

'*You* can decide that you'll all sit down here and rest, but what about me? What do you think the captain will say if I'm found just lazing around?'

These questions all require some support and assistance from the group and the response will have an effect on what the group is able to do next.

All of these uses of role can be adopted in one whole-group drama. In her book *Dorothy Heathcote: Drama as a Learning Medium* (National Education Association, Washington D.C., 1976), Betty Jane Wagner identifies a number of types of questions that Dorothy Heathcote has used to 'evoke class response' (p. 61). They include:

- questions that seek information or assess children's interest, including those that define the moment, and
  those that stimulate research in books or other documents, or suggest asking adults for information
- questions that supply information
- branching questions, which call for a group decision between alternative courses of action
- questions that control the class.

Information-seeking or interest-assessing questions could be of the following types:

—What shall we do a play about?
—What must you take with you?
—How many horses do we need?
—Do you remember what it was like the first day we arrived in this country?

The first sub-group of information-seeking questions (those that define the moment) comprise such questions as:

—What time of day is it?
—Exactly where are we in the town?
—What's the weather like?
—Where do you think we should put the stove?
—What problem is uppermost in our minds?

*Questioning is a vital teaching strategy when assisting children to structure their drama.*

The second sub-group (those that stimulate further research or the seeking of further information) will usually need to be answered before or after the drama. They could include:
—What did coaches look like in those days?
—How did people dress in Sydney in the 1840s?
—Should there be any system for organising this expedition?
—Would we have to pay for the flour?

Questions, instead of statements, can often be used to simultaneously impart information and focus on a problem the group faces or a task that has to be accomplished:
—When you have collected and sterilised the medical supplies you need, may I please inspect them at this table?
—How many litres of water should we take on this journey?
—You're actually going to ride that horse without a saddle?
—Well, why are you carrying your gun if you don't mean to use it?

Branching questions call for the group to make a decision between alternative courses of action. They have a very important function in determining the course of the action. As Wagner points out, by reducing the choices to two or three, they simplify the decisions that have to be taken, and are especially appropriate for children who may have trouble coping with open-ended choices. Here are some examples:
—Shall we be in the past, the present or the future?
—Shall we be all men or a group of men and women?
—Should we do a play about being in trouble or about helping people in trouble?
—Are we going to camp here and risk an attack by wild animals or should we go on even though we're exhausted?

Questions that control the class are perhaps the hardest to learn, yet are vitally important. The best strategy for using this type of question is to 'appear to be wondering aloud in a musing way or to be eager to get on with the action' (Wagner, p. 65). Some examples include:
—I wonder if we can keep the king from hearing us as we go past?
—Can you manage to keep working for a little longer?
—Do we need to do what our leader says?

# Drama as an integrating element in a related arts program

All the arts can be linked together in a program. An integrated arts program can give children a good deal of success in mastering skills, in developing their creative abilities and judgements, and in experiencing real enjoyment of the arts. Drama can be used to link music, visual art, craft and dance programs together. Drama also allows children to explore real-life applications of the arts, especially in areas such as design or ritual.

There is a variety of possible approaches. You might:
• use a story the class has been dramatising and develop it into a story told in dance. This dance can be linked to music, either of the children's own making or of their selection.
• develop characters from a picture the children like—perhaps a large 'realistic' painting, such as those by Australian artists like Tom Roberts or May Gibbs,

or an Aboriginal bark painting, which might depict a hunting or food-gathering scene. Children can use their own ideas to draw or paint a character based on what they have seen.

- use a piece of music and decide what sorts of action this music makes the group think might be taking place. Each child could describe the scene he or she finds the most exciting, and then paint the scene most enjoyed whilst listening to the music.

All of these approaches are quite simple but can cover a number of skills and concepts, such as using different levels and dynamics in dance, becoming more familiar with the concepts of pitch and duration in music, finding ways of using various media to create a visual image of an aural experience, and organising action and language to give a dramatic account of the ideas which other art forms can give the watcher or listener. Drama can be the point of entry into a larger program, or the culmination of a number of lessons where the class has researched, written and painted about an issue or idea. The understanding children have of issues and ideas is often shown in their drama, and so drama can be useful in the evaluation of a related arts program.

# Drama as an integrating element in a language program

Your language program can certainly be enriched by using drama as a stimulus for further exploration in reading and as a springboard for children's writing. Drama is a form of constructing stories and can be used as an alternative to narration. In order to find out more about people as characters in a story or drama, children might have to research extensively. If, for instance, the drama the children are concerned with is related to a group of scientists who want to see what is at the base of Antarctica, the class will need to do some reading about other explorers and scientists who have had the same ambitions. They might then need to make a list of the sorts of dangers they could face. (Lists like this can be scribed by the teacher for those groups not yet able to do their own writing. Alternatively, those with few reading skills can draw the lists or have them drawn for them.) They might need to compile an account of the sorts of difficulties they could encounter and write letters to others who might be able to help, e.g., to museums, government departments and international agencies. They might need to meet with people who have returned from expeditions. (This is where you can become Mawson and assist with some knowledge and experience.) The importance of exploring the implications of a story, rather than just telling a story, makes drama a more vivid language experience.

Explorers might also like to go to other places, such as Santa Claus's workshop, the place where teddy bears come from, under the sea, under the earth and into space. Exploring is a theme which most groups can use to follow an idea, and it certainly leads to a lot of discussion, reading, writing and drawing, so that records of the explorations can be kept.

Drama can also be used in language programs to extend children's uses of spoken language. There might be drama based on the need to persuade rather than bully, such as a drama where one group has to be persuaded to compromise about the boundary between two lands. Drama can also be used very effectively to move children past purely transactional language into language that is more poetic. A drama set in a fantasy situation may call for a very formal and accurate use of spoken language, which gives children some experience in using a formal tone of voice, and very formal sentence structure, requiring that they carefully choose the words which best describe their needs or wishes. Perhaps the leader of a tribe always addresses the people from high on a mountain top and therefore needs to speak clearly, simply and authoritatively. A lot of seven-year-olds might not otherwise get the chance to use such a tone or to find the descriptions needed.

# Drama as performance

Most children relish the opportunity to perform for others, whether it is for other class members, the whole school or a wider audience. Sometimes, the anticipation of the performance is the most exciting part! Children who have worked together on performances for special occasions remember those times as highlights of the school year. There are many different types of performances for children, but the most exciting of all are those which they make up, prepare and perform themselves. The place of dramatic performance in the primary school has been assured for a long time. Few schools or classes, however, make up their own plays, and the mad scramble for a suitable play for thirty, with at least twenty speaking parts, becomes an annual headache for many teachers. Consider how much easier such occasions can be if the class has been working on a number of different drama projects throughout the year, and children can choose from different types of performances.

Performance in the primary school should be an occasion for drawing together all the skills and knowledge which each class or individual has gained up to that point in the school year. Performance can take place at many times during the year and in a variety of informal ways. Some older groups might like to present a play for a younger class; other groups might like to perform a lunch-time pageant for the whole school. Look on performance as a frequent vehicle for expanding skills rather than as an arduous, much rehearsed, 'once-off' end-of-year task.

# Drama and personal development

Role play and drama games have often been used to assist in personal development programs. Through role play children can explore and solve problems which might one day become a real dilemma. Often they begin to gain an understanding of how groups in society work — how decisions are made by people who don't really agree with each other but who, for the common good, agree to a compromise. They can use role play to investigate their own reactions to problems they might already be encountering — what do they say to a bully, several years older, who demands money *with menace*? Even small children can work in a role-play situation, often with the teacher or another adult in one of the roles. Children can gain more understanding of a concept like sharing when they are in a position where they either need what someone else has, or they have to share in order to survive.

Drama games can help groups who might have some problems in getting along together. They can often be used as a starting point for a longer drama session — the object being to warm up the children before a movement lesson, or to provide an energising break in between long periods of concentration. Sheer fun and enjoyment can often be the objective in drama games, and they can be used on special occasions, such as picnics or class parties.

All drama experiences should be followed by a discussion which can help the group see the broader ramifications of their decisions and actions. If the decision has been to tell an adult about the bully, what will an individual do about a bully when there are no adults for protection? If someone has decided that he or she wants to keep all the bread and not ask for any apples, what happens when the bread is stale and inedible and those with the apples refuse to share because of the original decision? All these problems (and many others) can be the focus of drama which aims to assist personal and social development.

# Drama and movement

Movement is a major component in a drama program and can be linked to music, health studies and dance. Children can acquire strength, suppleness and grace through their movement work in drama. Movement is also a particularly valuable way into drama for those whose language development is poor. Children with speaking or hearing difficulties can find movement work especially enjoyable, as it gives them an opportunity to express themselves in another form and to develop a greater range of communication. Those who have difficulty with movement (such as children in calipers or braces) might need some assistance, but any child with even limited movement can join in many movement activities.

Movement can be a non-threatening approach to drama for those who are new to English and who do not yet have much confidence in speaking in another language. Spoken instructions do not need to be understood if a child can see all the others moving in a certain pattern or at a certain level. It can be pretty obvious what is going on and it is easy to join in. It may not always be clear *why* the movement lesson is going in the direction it does, but a drama lesson which concentrates on movement is much easier for these children than one which demands a lot of group interaction.

All children benefit from movement work which develops their awareness of visual signals in communication and helps them expand their own skills in this area. Movement gives children the opportunity to observe the ways in which others communicate with them in movement, and to think about ways they can make themselves better understood through movement.

# Short-term planning

A number of occasions may arise where short-term planning is the only approach available for you. For instance, you may realise that the children have progressed further in drama than you anticipated and they would like the opportunity to develop a big drama project for performance. Or something might happen in the school or the community which they would like to explore in their drama. All work needs planning, however, and it's best to have a few days in which to think about the ways in which you could approach such opportunities.

If the class has decided that they would like to perform for another class or for a school assembly, think about the different dramatic forms you could use. A movement sequence may be easier to develop than a play which they have to devise and rehearse. A play they have written themselves may need less rehearsal time than one written by an outside playwright.

If the class has decided they would like to do a whole group drama based on a local issue or incident, ask them to do some of the research and to bring in things they think might be needed: e.g., for a drama about prospecting, they could draw the maps, bring in the photos or collect the rocks.

Short-term planning is generally a response to an immediate need or interest and so can be beneficial. However, you should always try to keep your long-term objectives in mind, and see where the drama you suddenly have the opportunity to do fits in with what you and your colleagues have determined in the larger scale.

# Long-term planning

Most States provide some form of framework for drama in primary schools. The methods of distribution of such resources differ from State to State and from system to system. Get in touch with the education department in your State and find out what resources are available. Some Australian States, notably Tasmania, have drama advisers who are able to come and help the whole school and individual teachers to plan their work in drama. Others, like South Australia and New South Wales, have a framework or syllabus for drama, which consists of a broad outline of the principles underlying drama education and a set of more specific guidelines for drama in the classroom. Victorian teachers will find that there is an excellent source book for drama which can be purchased through the Education Department.

These sorts of resources will help you to plan for the long-term in your school. A long-term plan should include,
  • class/grade objectives for drama skills and concepts
  • a list of resources for drama in the school
  • individual/group programs that can be adapted
  • individual/group lesson plans that can be adapted
and eventually,
  • overall aims for drama in the school
  • a school policy for drama.
A long-term plan like this will help teachers who are new to the school, as well as teachers who want to see what their class might have done previously. It will also help determine the level of dramatic development of the children in the school generally and the level of each class. A long-term plan will help you to get together with colleagues in order to share ideas and approaches most suitable for your own needs and those of your children.

# 4 Drama and Movement from K-6

The inclusion of movement in a drama program gives children the opportunity to express themselves better in action, because movement activities develop their physical control and clarity of physical expression. Indeed, through movement they are able to become more effective in all aspects of communication. As they develop their movement skills, they gain an increased awareness of their physical abilities, which leads to positive feelings about themselves and other people. Movement also promotes trust and co-operation when working with others, especially when there is no sense of a critical audience.

Through movement, children can practise basic locomotor and non-locomotor skills. They develop their understanding of concepts basic to movement, such as time, space, energy and spatial relationships. This understanding is related to their improvisation as well as to activities which may need more direct instruction. And, as with other aspects of drama, movement requires children to participate in solving problems as well as in finding expression for ideas and feelings. Children experiment with movement by exploring the ways they can move, individually or with others.

Movement provides a link between thought and language by giving children a medium for self-expression before they may have the skills to express themselves fully through speaking and writing. Children often use movement to express what cannot be communicated properly in words. For example, when 'ice-cream' is mentioned, the pre-school child will often show enthusiasm through hand clapping and jumping; a child having difficulties with language may show frustration by aggressive behaviour. A structured movement program is very useful with E.S.L. children, slow learners and children with special needs, as it assists them to improve a powerful means of expression.

The basic skills and concepts related to movement are shown below.

Figure 4.1

| MOVEMENT SKILLS | | MOVEMENT CONCEPTS | | | |
|---|---|---|---|---|---|
| *Locomotor* | *Non-locomotor* | *Time* | *Space* | *Energy* | *Relationship* |
| walk | sway | fast | personal | heavy | alone |
| run | swing | slow | space | light | pairs |
| creep | rock | short | common | | groups |
| crawl | twist | long | space | | together |
| roll | stretch | | levels | | contrasting |
| slide | curl | | shape | | harmonious |
| jump | bend | | | | |
| hop | | | | | |

# Levels of progression in movement

Children who are beginning movement need a lot of activities in the introduction of each movement skill and concept. Children should become familiar with these skills and concepts before putting language to their actions. At this level they

☐ develop the locomotor movements of
- walking
- running
- creeping
- crawling
- rolling
- sliding
- hopping
- jumping

☐ develop the non-locomotor movements of
- swaying
- swinging
- rocking
- twisting
- curling
- bending

☐ are introduced to the movement concepts of
- time
- space
- energy

☐ work individually, in pairs, and sometimes in groups

☐ interact with others co-operatively and with trust

☐ take on simple roles from real life, fantasy and literature

☐ develop short movement sequences using a combination of two or three movements and concepts.

For children with some drama experience, concepts and skills introduced earlier need to be reinforced with challenging combinations of movements. The children will be better able to use language to describe their movements. At this level they

☐ consolidate locomotor and non-locomotor movements already introduced

☐ develop the locomotor movements of
- gallop
- trot
- leap
- skip

☐ consolidate the concepts of time, space and energy
☐ are introduced to the idea of relationships in movement
☐ make decisions and solve problems in a group
☐ use movements for different effects
☐ develop longer movement sequences using character and plot, and combinations of movement skills and concepts.

Once children have lots of drama experience, they reinforce all that has been previously developed. They are able to apply skills and concepts to new situations when developing their ideas into movement. These children have good movement control and may even discover new combinations of movements through experimentation. Character and plot are important, as the children spend more time forming their own ideas into movement pieces for performance. At this level they

☐ consolidate movement skills and concepts through complex combinations of movement
☐ develop contrasting and complementary movement relationships in their work
☐ form their ideas into challenging movement pieces involving character and plot
☐ work well in groups
☐ explore abstract ideas in their movement work.

## *Planning for movement lessons*

In all movement work your aims should be to explain and clarify body movements, to encourage the children to discover more movements and to develop and encourage creativity through movement.

When children are first starting movement, it's best to let them explore their own movement repertoire without restriction, apart from safety precautions (such as finding their own space when kicking, or not touching anyone when running in a group). This helps the children to become aware of their bodies and of the movements they already have. Music is a useful accompaniment for these activities. Once children have had many experiences through physical action, they are more able to use language to describe the action and apply it to new situations.

Establish a positive atmosphere and show your enthusiasm by joining in. It's also important for you and your children to exchange ideas freely. Set up routines to promote the smooth running of each lesson. At the beginning you can get each child to take off shoes and socks and sit in a personal space. Use music to signal this. Relaxing activities at the beginning and end of each lesson settle the children into the lesson and calm them down at the end. A word such as 'freeze' or a sound from a musical instrument can be used to signal 'stop'. The time of day is also important for movement activities. Generally, the end of the day is not a good time, because the children are tired and movement requires a lot of energy.

It is better to start with individual movement responses before planning for pair work and then small group work. Children need to become familiar with what their own bodies can do and to develop the appropriate social skills before working with others.

The process of introducing movement skills and concepts is similar for children of all ages who have had no experience. However, older children are more likely to acquire and use the names and descriptions of each skill and concept as it is introduced, whereas younger children can only be expected to remember this vocabulary after many movement activities. A chart listing the movements and concepts as they are introduced will help children draw on previous experiences. Figure 4.2 is an example of a chart devised for children with some experience. Children can work over the chart in horizontal or vertical lines, or in diagonals, or else choose skills and concepts at random. They can decide on a story they would like to tell using the chosen movements, or decide on the story first and then choose the appropriate movements.

Figure 4.2

*What movements are you going to explore today?*

| Movement | Time | Space | Energy |
|----------|------|-------|--------|
| slide | fast | low | light |
| jump | slow | high | heavy |
| twist | long | big shape | smooth |
| curl | short | small shape | jerky |

A group of children who are developing a movement sequence on machines could choose the contrasting movements of twist/long/big shape/smooth, and curl/short/small shape/jerky to show the different working parts of their machine.

Children who are just beginning may have only one, two or three columns in their chart. They may all be movement columns, with no concept columns, depending on what they have done. Experienced children will have four or more columns, with the addition of a relationship column and the dividing of concept areas into a number of columns (e.g., four columns could be used for space — level, floor pattern, shape and direction).

In order to evaluate your movement program, you must continually observe the children and record your observations, so as to:

- determine each child's level of ability
- identify each child's specific needs, whether they be extension or remediation in particular areas
- assess whether activities suited the children's interests and levels of ability.

When you are programming for a movement lesson, consider whether you have gone through these steps:

- determining the needs and interests of the children
- planning for introductory activities in order to warm up
- deciding which basic movements and concepts you want to introduce
- deciding whether there are any movements and/or concepts you need to revise
- choosing an idea or theme around which to plan the activities
- gathering together any stimulus materials, such as music, art, stories and poetry; scarves, ribbons, hoops and boxes
- making sure you have left time for discovery and improvisation by the children
- providing opportunities for reflection
- providing opportunities for evaluation.

*Movement is an important part of communication.*

# Ideas for developing movement skills and concepts

Any movement lesson should include a number of movement skills and concepts and some awareness activities.

## Body awareness activities

Children need to be aware of their body parts in order to move their bodies expressively. They become aware by moving each part in isolation and in combination with other parts. Here are some suggestions for early awareness activities.

☐ Sitting on the floor without shoes, the children move their toes in as many ways as possible. Freeze. Then they move their ankles in as many ways as possible. Freeze. They continue to freeze the moving body part and experiment with the next body part all the way up the body: e.g., knee, hips, back, shoulders, arms, head.

As a variation, try adding the next body part without freezing, until the whole body is moving.

☐ The children imagine that there is a mosquito biting them on the forehead. Without using their hands they must move to make it go away. It settles on another part of the body and they try to make it go away again.

☐ Mirror work—the children in pairs choose one of each pair to be the leader. The other follows the leader's actions as closely as possible. They swap over. Afterwards discuss the actions that were easier/harder to copy.
     As variations:  • limit the actions to one or two body parts
                              • pretend to be looking into distorting mirrors at a fun fair.

☐ Walking Tip—the children walk around the room. On a prearranged signal they have to see how many elbows/backs/knees they can tip before the signal to freeze. Each child tries to make it harder for the other children by evading them.

## *Basic movements*

Children need to develop and consolidate basic movement skills when they are beginning drama. Here are some activities to develop these basic skills.

**Walk**
  • on a hot footpath
  • on broken glass
  • through long grass
  • on soft carpet
  • through mud
  • on the moon.
Think of some other places to walk and make up a story to go with them. Add sound effects.

**Run**
  • using as much space as possible
  • using as little space as possible
  • like different animals
  • changing directions
  • as if it were very hot or cold.
Find or create some music that would suit these activities.

**Crawl**
  • along the top of a very narrow high wall
  • facing the floor
  • facing the ceiling
  • through a small hole that is almost too small to fit through.
Create a maze of dark tunnels to crawl through in the classroom. Then, as a class, decide
  • who you are
  • where you are
  • why you are there
  • what is happening.
Act out the story, and perhaps record it in writing and drawing.

**Roll**
- like a steam-roller
- like a paint roller going along the wall and around corners
- like a blind being pulled up quickly and pulled down slowly.

Find as many different ways to roll as possible. Create a sequence of sounds to go with the rolls.

**Jump**
- as high as possible
- as low as possible
- like a kangaroo
- like a footballer heading the ball
- in fast or slow motion.

Children in groups choose leaders. The leader is a flea trainer and the others are the fleas. Each group prepares a circus act using all the different jumps the clever fleas can perform.

Here are some activities to develop non-locomotor skills.

**Twist**
- like clothes in the washing machine
- to burst balloons which are falling from the sky. There may be pins on your shoulders and hips to burst them.

Find some good twisting music for daily fitness or a class dance.

**Turn**
- around on the spot
- to face the other way
- different parts of the body
- like a corkscrew pulling out a cork.

Play 'follow the leader' using these different turns.

Other movement skills shown in Figure 4.1 can be treated in similar ways. To extend the children's movement skills, ask them to develop sequences and stories using a combination of movements. For instance, a sequence such as run, jump and curl can be used to tell a story about an escape—running across a paddock, jumping over a rock and hiding behind it in a curled-up position.

# Activities to develop an understanding of the concept of time

In movement time refers to how long it takes to get from one place or position to another. A pathway can be *long* or *short*, and a movement can be *fast* or *slow*. A movement sequence may use different durations in order to create interesting effects. The concept of time can be developed by activities such as follow.

☐ Get the children in pairs, and blindfold one in each pair. The seeing partner then takes the blindfolded one:
- on a short route in the room
- on a long route in the room

Swap roles and then discuss which activities were fast/slow.

☐ Choose a course for the children to move along. Ask them to:
  • move along it as quickly as possible
  • move along it as slowly as possible
  • crawl very close to the ground
  • walk on tiptoe.
Time each activity and discuss how the different movements made a difference to the time it took to complete the course.

☐ Let the children find movements that are:
  • fast
  • slow
Then each can show another which movements took the longest/shortest time to do.

☐ Let the children find different pathways that take:
  • a long time to complete
  • a short time to complete.
Then they can try drawing the different ways they moved, labelling them fast and slow.

# Activities to develop an understanding of the concept of space

## Personal and common space

Establish the concept of personal and common space in the early stages of a movement program. Respect for personal and common space makes a difference to the quality of the children's responses.

Children need to understand that everyone has his or her own personal space, which is the space that surrounds each person and separates that person from others. The space that we share with others is the common space. Here are some ideas for activities to develop an understanding of these spaces.

☐ Individual movement activities can be done within a visible boundary, such as a hoop or a ring of chalk. Once children are familiar with working in their personal space, plan activities that allow them to move outside their personal space into the common space and then back to their personal space again. As children demonstrate an ability to use both personal and common space, the visible boundaries can be replaced with imaginary ones.

☐ Play some rhythmic dance music and ask the class to move to the music in their personal space. When you call 'share', everyone moves out of their personal space and dances around the room with the others. When you call 'alone', the children remain within their personal space to dance.

☐ Half the class at a time move around the room blindfolded. By paying attention to aural signals, they stay in their personal space and do not share that space with anybody. If they touch they are out. So that everyone can concentrate, there should be no talking.

## Levels

The introduction of levels is important in order to extend the children's movement responses early in a drama program. They come to realise that movements do not always start from a standing position. Levels can be *high, medium* or *low*, and the following examples will give some ideas for developing an understanding of them.

☐ Low levels are:
- scrubbing or polishing a floor
- picking up pieces of a broken vase
- digging weeds out of a garden
- building a sand castle.

☐ Medium levels are:
- playing the piano
- making your bed
- mowing the lawn
- clearing the table.

☐ High levels are:
- painting the ceiling
- pulling yourself up by a rope
- casting a fishing line
- waving to someone across the park.

☐ All levels are:
- pulling a blind down and following it up
- painting a wall
- putting books back on library shelves.

## Shape

Shape refers to the body shapes we make as we move. It gives children more interesting ways to move and more expressive means to get their ideas across. Basic body shapes are *pointed, flat, round* and *twisted*. They can be *large, middle-sized* or *small*. Here are two ideas for developing the children's awareness of shape.

*Children understand the concept of levels early in a drama program.*

☐ The children lie on the floor in as small a shape as possible. They become balloons and inflate. When the balloons are big they hold that shape. Get them to feel how different it is to the small balloon. You can then go around the room with a pin and burst the balloons one by one. The children hold the small shape again.

☐ With the children in pairs, one child decides on a shape and models the other into it, either by talking or physically moving the body parts. (The shapes can be chosen from a list the class has made.) The children who are the 'sculptures' have their eyes closed and try to guess what shapes they have become.

## Direction

Without guidance, children use movements that go mostly forwards and backwards. Making them conscious of other directions increases the scope of their movements. You need to make them aware that movements can take different directions — not only *forwards and backwards*, but *sideways, in diagonals* or *right and left*. They can go *to and from, under and over, up and down, between, around, above and below* and *into and out of*. Children can also take direct or indirect routes in their movements. Ideas for developing some of these directions are:

• taking part in a tug of war (forwards and backwards)
• passing a football and covering the person with the ball (side to side)
• walking along the row to your seat at the cinema (sideways)
• hurrying to get to school (direct)
• visiting friends on the way to school because there is plenty of time (indirect).

## Floor patterns

An awareness of floor patterns also extends the scope of the children's movements. It shows them that movements do not always have to be in straight lines. Floor patterns are an introduction to dance patterns (such as weaving patterns in folk dances and zig zag patterns in tribal dances) which may be explored as children gain experience. Patterns can be *curved, zig zag, broken* or *straight*. Here are some ideas for making children aware of different floor patterns.

☐ Ask the children to make patterns in the sand pit with their feet as if they were
• a snail
• a kangaroo
• a dog chasing its tail
• a runaway robot that keeps running into walls.

☐ Record patterns on large sheets of paper. This might be done by individual children with paint on the soles of their feet. Describe the patterns and write down their names.

☐ In groups the children form the shapes of letters or numbers as they are called out. Another child or yourself can be the caller.

# *Activities to develop an understanding of the concept of energy*

Energy changes the quality of movements, making them more expressive and adding contrast to movement sequences. Energy can be *light, heavy/strong, jerky* or *smooth*. Here are some ideas for developing an awareness of energy in movement.

☐ Ask the children to pass imaginary objects around a circle — such as a butterfly, a feather, a large rough rock and a heavy boot. The children show whether their movements need to be strong or light to accommodate the object.

☐ In pairs or small groups, the children can explore
  - being lost in a dark cave
  - being a large lizard crashing through the bush
  - walking on the moon
  - becoming burglars robbing a house
  - the actions of a strong man at the circus
  - the movements of a robot that stops and starts
  - a snake's movements.

## Understanding relationships

All movements have relationships, whether they are related to ideas, to the movements of others or to the movements of other body parts, and whether they are *harmonious* or *contrasting*. These relationships occur in all the skill and concept areas, and it is a good idea to make children aware of them as they develop and extend their movement repertoire. Being aware of these relationships will help children develop structure in their movement sequences, particularly for performance pieces. For instance, a sequence might start with harmonious movements, build up tension with contrasting movements and then resolve the tension with harmonious movements again. Here are some activities to help make children aware of relationships.

☐ Ask the children to find movements that are opposite to
  - a slow heavy walk
  - a fast jerky bend
  - a curved smooth run
  - a big straight leap.

☐ Children in pairs add a movement to go with one already started by their partner. Pairs can join up to develop a group exercise on a theme, such as a particular type of machine. One person starts with a movement, and the others join in one by one with complementary movements, adding sound effects.

## Action words

Using action words during movement lessons can help the children to express their movements more effectively. Such words as *push, pull, press, flick, punch, float, wring, dab, slash* and *glide* are effective.[1] For example, the word *push* will help children explore a heavy, long and direct movement.

All of these movement activities are provided as stimuli for further development of ideas. Use them to sequence your movement program. The best sequence in the introduction of the basic movements would be similar to the order shown in Figure 4.1. After they are introduced, vary them to extend the children's skills.

[1] These words are cited by Rudolf Laban in *The Mastery of Movement* (4th edition), Macdonald and Evans, London, 1980.

For example:
- combine two non-locomotor movements, such as stretch and turn;
- extend further by adding a movement concept, such as space, so that the children stretch and turn at high and low levels.

Introduce the concepts of time, space and energy concurrently with the basic movement skills when the children are ready.

With all these activities it is often a good idea to provide models for the children. Half the class might observe the others as they take turns to do the movement activity. Alternatively you could make a video of the work they have done. You can then take the opportunity to draw the children's attention to movements that display physical skill or an understanding of a movement concept. Take time to reflect and discuss any successes and difficulties during and after the movement lesson. This will help in the planning of new activities.

# Integrating movement with a music program

By combining movement skills and concepts with music you are able to integrate music and drama. Movement skills and concepts can be taught in combination with the musical skills and concepts of singing, playing, organising sound and listening.

Children can gain their first musical experiences through movement because it allows them to become familiar with music concepts in action before developing the language for them. Here are some ideas for doing this.

### Body Awareness
- Ask the children to touch selected body parts to music so that they can experience beat.
- Give the children experience in rhythm by getting them to use body percussion to play the rhythm of a favourite song.

### Locomotion
- Provide the children with some music that has accents throughout—either recorded or played by you on a percussion instrument. Ask them to walk to the music but jump whenever they hear a sound emphasised.
- Let the children experience a variety of sound sources and ask them to fit sounds to their movements, e.g., sway, twist, roll and slide.
- Ask the children to put actions to a known song, such as 'Baa Baa Black Sheep', in order to experience phrasing.

### Awareness of Time
- Let the children experience tempo in music by walking fast or slow according to the speed of the music being played.

### Awareness of Space
- Combine high and low movement levels with musical pitch by playing or singing high and low notes while the children respond in movement.
- You can provide experience of movement direction and of recognising different patterns in music by asking the children to walk forwards when they hear 'Hot Cross Buns', and backwards when they hear 'Here we go round the Mulberry Bush'. Make sure you choose songs that suit the children.

### Awareness of Energy

- Play loud and soft music, either recorded or of your own making. Ask the children to respond to these dynamics by making heavy or light movements.

As children gain experience in movement you will be able to combine movement skills and concepts to present musical concepts, as in the following activities.

### Locomotion and Awareness of Space

- Choose music with a steady beat and ask the children to change movements and energy levels to suit other features of the music. They can change direction each time the volume of the music changes.

- Children slide at low and medium levels to show long sounds for their whole duration. Ask them to find suitable movements for short sounds.

### Locomotion and Awareness of Time and Energy

- The children walk with heavy to light energy levels to show 'gradually getting faster'. Each child plays his or her own accompanying music on a percussion instrument. Reverse the sequence to show 'gradually getting slower'.

Children with lots of experience in movement can use music to enhance their work, or as a stimulus on which to base their work. They have control over their body movements, and are able to use more complex movement combinations to express their ideas or interpret the music they hear. Here is an example of what they could do.

*An integrated music and drama program is both practical and fun.*

### Locomotion and Awareness of Space, Energy and Time

- Make up a dance with the children based on a theme or story and the movements that the music suggests. Design it so that the dancers move from common to personal space within the dance and change direction each time the music changes. The dance should reflect the energy and timing of the music. This will develop understanding of the musical concepts of duration, dynamics, tone colour and structure.

Whenever you are about to teach a musical concept, examine ways for the children to experience it through movement first. Movement is a link between thought and language, and so it is a great help in introducing children to musical ideas.

# Movement, health studies and imagination

Drama and health studies both aim to develop skill in basic movements and an understanding of time, space and energy in order to foster body awareness and self-expression. They differ in the emphasis given to role and plot in drama.

Drama and health studies can be integrated in a movement program if it aims to develop:

- body awareness
- locomotion
- spatial awareness
- hand-eye and foot-eye coordination
- rhythm and timing
- an understanding of role and plot
- imagination and self-expression.

Providing children with roles, themes and fantasy to illustrate and explore different movements makes the development of movement skills more meaningful. Children can draw ideas from past experiences in order to explore new ground. An integrated program emphasises the use of imagination and is very effective in developing self-expression. And children enjoy this approach more than a mechanical sequence of movement activities.

## Roles from literature

A good way of achieving integration is by exploring characters in literature through movement. New skills and concepts can be introduced by getting the children to take on roles of favourite characters — walking just how they walk, doing tricks just as they do, and getting out of sticky situations or using the same movements as them. It's a good idea to look out for stories which have characters with obvious movements for the children to use as models. This sort of interpretation also helps in the children's comprehension of stories and so integrates with reading as well. Here are some examples of books that can be used in this way.

*The Rainbow Serpent* retold by Dick Roughsey and Percy Trezise (Collins). The Rainbow Serpent's search for his lost tribe conjures up wonderful images of slithering and sliding which children love to imitate, and so this book makes a good introduction to those movements.

*Bertie the Bear* by Pamela Allen (Nelson). The action-packed illustrations of Bertie escaping from the bear can be a great stimulus when you introduce leaping to your children.

*Angelo* by Quentin Blake (Penguin). This story is about a young girl who runs away to become a circus performer. Angelo's antics lend themselves to a combination of basic movements such as balancing, turning, bending, stretching and walking at different levels. Movement sequences using balance as the focus can be worked into circus acts (you can use skipping ropes on the ground as tight ropes). Carnival music and costumes complete the effect.

*The Lion, the Witch and the Wardrobe* by C. S. Lewis (Collins/Puffin). The forces of good and evil in this book can be represented in movement by children with lots of experience, either as a class or in groups. Before improvising in movement, the children explore the characters in detail, discussing and listing their physical characteristics, personal traits, the situations they find themselves in and what they represent in the story. At this level they have a large movement repertoire for their interpretation of the story, and you may be quite amazed at the work they produce. The story might be worked into a performance by rehearsal and by creating music and costumes to go with it.

## *Themes*

You can also base movements on themes being studied in other curriculum areas. This is an excellent way of integrating other subjects with drama and movement — particularly social studies, natural science and language themes. Here are some ideas.

- A theme on *Ourselves* can start the children exploring their body parts and how each one moves. Movements should be based on particular actions, e.g., 'What movements do I make when I'm eating, putting on my clothes or cleaning my teeth?' Comparisons might follow: e.g., 'Do I move in a different way to somebody else when I do this?'

- A theme on *How I Express Myself* might use movement to express contrasting emotions, e.g., sadness/happiness. You'll find that children will discover contrasting movements to go with these emotions: for instance, when exploring sadness they may use a heavy, slow, walking movement at a low to medium level, but when exploring happiness they use a light, fast run at a medium to high level. This type of activity helps make children aware of how we express ourselves through movement in everyday life. A follow-up would be to observe people in the street and try to analyse their movements and feelings.

- A theme on *Colour* and how it affects us requires more abstract thinking and an extensive movement repertoire. In groups the children choose a colour to explore through movement. They discuss in detail the feelings this colour has for them. These feelings will probably vary from person to person, but the differences will add interest to the sequence, with contrasting movements introducing tension. The movement chart outlined earlier in Figure 4.1 will help in analysing the movements. The groups should be given time to develop an interesting sequence through improvising and refining, and by adding costumes and music they can extend their work into a performance.

# Fantasy

Fantasy is another source of ideas for movement, as the following ideas will show.

- You can develop spatial awareness in the early stages by using a large box or tunnel as a dark cave. Each child explores the space he or she is in by feeling forwards/backwards, sideways, in front/behind, up/down and in and out of the cave. Tactile objects (such as rubber for slime and fake fur for bats) are an added stimulus and could provide a way of assessing the children's understanding of space. For instance, you will know if children understand 'behind' by what they say they can feel when you ask, 'What's blocking your escape from behind?'

- An obstacle course set up to practise leaping, balancing and turning with light energy at high and medium levels might be turned into a space station on the moon.

- A box of fantasy cards can be set up in the classroom where more advanced groups with some spare time can go for ideas to develop into movement sequences. The cards should be written as a joint effort by everyone in the class. Children at this more advanced stage should also be given a lot of freedom to develop their own ideas. In groups they can decide on a fantasy world that they want to explore through movement. Drawing on their movement repertoire, and with teacher assistance if needed, they should be given opportunities to polish their work into performance.

There are many possibilities for developing role and plot into movement sequences, and you should always be on the look out for new ideas to motivate the children into movement.

# Some sample movement lessons

The three series of sample lessons described below incorporate many of the ideas and suggestions examined earlier in this chapter. They provide examples of how you can structure and sequence activities in order to introduce or consolidate skills and concepts, either individually or in combination.

The series are graded according to the amount of experience children have had in movement and drama work, and not necessarily according to their ages or level of intellectual development. It is quite possible, for example, for a Year 5 class to be having lessons similar to those in Series 1, while the Year 4 class next door is doing more advanced work.

## Series 1: for children beginning movement work

**Lesson 1**

**Basic movements**
Introduce: stretch, walk.

**Movement concepts**
Introduce: space—high level.

*Activities*
1. Run a beater up the high notes of a tuned percussion instrument such as a glockenspiel. Ask the children to listen and:

- stretch as high as they can
- walk, making themselves as tall as they can.

2. Give the children time to experiment with high, stretch walks. Ask them to find activities they might do in real life that use high, stretch walks. As the children give their ideas the whole class tries out each activity. Some ideas might be:
   - painting the ceiling of the classroom
   - looking for a book along the top shelf of the library.

3. Use one of these stretching activities to relax the children at the end of this lesson. You could, for example, ask them each to take a book from that top shelf of the library and browse through it quietly. They could tell a partner what the book is about.

## Lesson 2

*Basic movements*
Revise: stretch, walk.

*Movement concepts*
Revise: space — high level.
Introduce: space — low level.

*Activities*
1. Use the stretch/walk suggestions from the last lesson as the children walk around the room to warm up.
2. Find ways to stretch that are not up high. Discuss with the children the stretches they find.
3. Choose a child who is stretching at a low level as an example for the class to follow.
4. Discuss the level the child is using. Then give the other children time to experiment with their own stretches at this level.
5. At the end of this lesson let the children rest, stretching out on the floor.

## Lesson 3

*Basic movements*
Revise: stretch, walk.

*Movement concepts*
Revise: space — high and
              low levels.

*Activities*
1. Ask the children to move around the room to music such as chords (three notes) played on the piano. On your call they walk, either stretching up high or down low.
2. Try a movement at a low level that is very different from the stretch. Give the children time to share their discovered movements.
3. Choose a child who is curling as a model for the others. If no child is curling, demonstrate the movement yourself.
4. Let the children experiment with curling and stretching at this low level.
5. Divide the class into pairs. Each pair discusses what creature (imaginary or real) could be stretching and curling close to the ground, and then decides on another creature that walks and stretches up tall. Each child takes the part of one of the creatures and makes up a story about it.
6. The children show their stories to the class.

### Evaluation points
- Have children show an ability to express their ideas through the movements that were introduced and revised?
- Were the children able to work in pairs?
- Did the children display imaginative ideas?
- Did the activities suit each child's level of ability?
- Did any children start to explore new movements?
- Use the answers to these questions to plan new activities.

## Series 2: for children with some experience in movement

In this series of lessons, skills and concepts introduced earlier in the program are consolidated through an interpretation of literature. The story or book you choose as the basis of your lessons will, of course, depend on the age and interests of the children in your class. Older children may enjoy working with a video, such as a rock clip.

### Lesson 1

*Basic movements*
Consolidate: running.

*Movement concepts*
Consolidate: energy—light.

*Activities*
1. Read 'Jack and the Beanstalk' or tell the story yourself.
2. Discuss with the children what movement Jack used when escaping from the giant. Why did he move in this way?
3. Suggest that the children try running like Jack. Form them into pairs which act out the giant chasing Jack. Swap roles.
4. Choose a pair to run like each of the characters. The other children close their eyes and listen for the giant and Jack. Ask how they knew who was who— e.g., by the heavy or light footsteps.
5. Ask each pair to experiment with the different footsteps.

### Lesson 2

*Basic movements*
Consolidate: creeping.

*Movement concepts*
Consolidate: time—fast
                       slow.

*Activities*
1. Ask the children to lie on the floor and think about:
   - when people would creep slowly
   - when people would run fast.
2. Get thoughts shared around the class. Demonstrate these thoughts through movement.
3. Read or tell 'Jack and the Beanstalk' again. Ask the children to listen for:
   - someone creeping
   - someone going fast
   - someone going slowly.

4. Record the findings on the board. Discuss why Jack was creeping and why Jack and the giant were fast or slow at different times.
5. Ask the children to experiment with these movements while you read or tell part of the story to them.

## Lesson 3

| *Basic movements* | *Movement concepts* |
|---|---|
| Consolidate: running, creeping. | Consolidate: energy — light |
| | heavy |
| | time — fast |
| | slow. |

### Activities
1. Ask the children to move around the room to music. Percussion instruments are good for suggesting different ways of moving, e.g., running fast or slow.
2. Discuss these movements and list them on a chart.
3. Tell the complete story while the children portray it through movement, using fast running, slow creeping and heavy and light footsteps.

### Evaluation points
- Was each child able to interpret the movements in the story?
- Did any children find other movements in the story?
- Did I make the purpose of the lesson clear to the children?
- Were the activities well sequenced for the children's level of development?
- Were all the children's ideas valued?
- Did the choice of stimulus material help the children with their movements?

# Series 3: for children experienced in movement and drama work

In these lessons movement skills and concepts that have been introduced earlier are consolidated in activities which make considerable demands on the children's ability to think creatively and to translate their ideas into movement.

## Lesson 1

### Aim
To consolidate movement skills and related concepts that have been introduced and practised earlier in the program.

### Activities
1. Ask the children to stand in their own space and find their centre of balance by leaning forwards and backwards and by circling around, using the soles of their feet to keep balanced. Ask them to feel and be aware of the support they are getting from their toes, and from the ball, sides and heel of each foot.
2. Form the children into pairs. Members of each pair take turns to mirror each other's movements.
3. In pairs, the children tell each other about something terrible that has happened

to them in the last week. Each child then tells back his or her partner's story without changing any details or leaving any out.

4.  Still in pairs, the children relate their own stories in movement. Each child then portrays his or her partner's story, reproducing the movements as exactly as possible. Afterwards the children discuss whether anything was left out.

## Lesson 2

### Aim
To consolidate movement skills and related concepts that have been introduced and practised earlier in the program.

### Activities
1.  In pairs, the children touch each other's hands and try to remember what they feel like. Blindfold all the children and re-form them into small groups. The children then try to find their former partners by feeling the hands of the others in their group.
    Repeat, this time getting the children to feel each other's faces.
2.  In pairs, the children tell each other about something very important that has happened to them.
3.  Each child then interprets his or her partner's story in movement and the children discuss whether the movement reflected the feelings originally aroused by what happened.
4.  If the movement did not capture the right feelings, the pair talk further and the child interpreting the story tries again.

## Lesson 3

### Aims
To consolidate movement skills and related concepts that have been introduced and practised earlier in the program.
To consolidate the idea of contrasting and harmonious relationships.

### Activities
1.  Divide the children into groups and ask each group to decide on an occasion for a still photograph showing a group of people who get on well together. The groups then work out poses for their photographs.
2.  This time each photograph will be of a group of people who don't get on together — e.g., quarrelling brothers and sisters, or a group of adults arguing.
3.  Each group shows its poses to the rest of the class and the class discusses how the pictures showed contrast or harmony.
4.  Each group uses movement to create a 'feeling machine'. Try to get the children to use contrasting movements in their machines to portray a range of contrasting feelings. When the machine is working the children can add sound effects.
5.  Ask each group to create a 'single feeling machine', using a sequence of movements that are harmonious. Again, sound effects can be added to enhance the feeling suggested.
6.  Encourage the children to refine and rehearse their machines and then perform them for the rest of the class.

*'Mirrors' requires concentration and rapport with a partner.*

### Evaluation points
- Did the children use a variety of movement skills and concepts to portray different ideas and feelings?
- Did the children work well in pairs and groups?
- Were the activities well sequenced?
- Did the children show an understanding of contrasting and complementary movements in their work?
- What activities would build on and extend the skills practised in these lessons?

# 5 Drama and the Language Program

In the opening chapter we considered how important dramatic experience is in the child's early language development. At school, drama can and should continue to play a vital role in the acquisition and practice of more advanced speaking and listening skills, and in reading and writing. Developing language skills is part of drama: most of the time children are engaged in drama they are practising language and extending their ability to communicate clearly and effectively.

Drama is a valuable teaching strategy in a reading program. Stepping into the shoes of favourite characters from stories and books and living through the experiences of those characters can enhance children's appreciation of the written word and their awareness of such literary concepts as plot, structure and tension. These experiences flow into their writing and provide a fund of ideas for their own stories.

Language and drama programs are complementary in the benefits they offer children: drama is perhaps the best means of practising and extending language skills, and proficiency in language will obviously improve the quality of the children's drama. However, it is important to bear in mind that drama has its own special set of skills, understanding and knowledge. A child who is an accomplished reader, writer or speaker will not necessarily be skilled in drama.

It may therefore be helpful to summarise here the needs and developing skills of children working through a drama program. Children who are beginning drama need to —

- develop belief in the roles that they take
- learn to work with others in the drama
- begin to realise the value of their own ideas in drama
- develop the skills of speech and movement in order to provide appropriate language and action for the roles they take
- be provided with models of make-believe situations in poetry and prose
- base their drama on simple characterisations from favourite stories and poems as well as on real life.

As they develop confidence in drama, children are increasingly aware of the importance of speech and movement in the development of roles. Their roles become more original and believable as they experiment with the various ways their characters might react in different situations. And, as they develop social skills, they are better able to work in groups within a drama. With some experience in drama, children —

- work in role for longer periods
- make decisions and solve problems
- use the skills of movement and speech for different effects
- begin to use their own ideas in developing plays, perhaps using characters from other sources
- polish their ideas into written form and performance
- begin to publish their plays and stories.

Children who have had a great deal of experience in drama will have been exposed to many literary models and are now able to use their own ideas for developing characters and plot. They have greater skill of speech and movement; they understand tension and problem solving, and have a broader general knowledge from which to draw new ideas. Children at this more advanced level need to be given opportunities to —

- develop their ideas through role and plot
- become aware of developing and resolving complications within their plays
- collaborate with others to solve problems
- refine their work and present it to others in performance
- publish their plays and stories
- interpret the work of their peers
- be involved in drama for extended periods.

# Speaking, listening and drama

The ability to listen as well as to speak is as essential in drama as it is in other forms of communication. Without active listening there can be no true interaction between people in a conversation or characters in a play.

The following ideas, graded from those for children beginning drama to those for children who are experienced, can be used at different stages of a drama program to help children develop their skills in speaking and listening.

### Performing names
Invite the children to perform their own name to the class. Ask them to consider its length, how the name makes them feel and the sounds that would suit it. Get them to practise it and ask someone else what they think of it. You could also tape each name performance and play it back to see if any of the children want to make changes. Then they should perform it for the class.

As a variation the children can use the names of cars, fruit or vegetables.

### Finding different sounds
Ask the children to use their voices to create as many different sounds as possible. Some examples are:
- a happy sound
- an angry sound
- a low sound
- a jerky sound
- a loud sound
- a soft sound.

Decide what each sound is about. Choose four of the sounds and repeat them one after the other while the children put movements to them. Alternatively the children can do this in pairs or groups.

## Sound shapes
The children draw shapes on cardboard and show each other how the shapes would sound. They add movements to the sounds. As a variation half the class could make the sounds while the others respond with movements.

## Sound pictures
Choose a large picture – e.g., from a stimulus kit – and show it to the class. Discuss what is in the picture and what is happening. Individually or in groups, the children can then create the sounds they imagine would be in the picture if it came to life.

## How do I feel?
The children take it in turns to say the same sentence – e.g., 'I've got something for you' – with each child trying to suggest a different feeling. The feelings suggested might include sadness, anger, boredom, happiness, pride, surprise or fright. The other children try to guess the feeling each child is suggesting.

## Pair discussion
In pairs, the children decide on a topic they feel strongly about – perhaps something they really like or dislike. In turn they each talk on their topic for about 30 seconds. As they get better, you can devise a selection of topics for them to choose out of a hat.

## Imagine if . . .
Ask the children in pairs to make up conversations (about 30 seconds long) which might take place between:
- a caterpillar and the leaf it is about to eat
- a paint brush and some paints (the brush could be complaining about how dirty the paints made it)
- a pencil and the paper it is writing on
- a pear and a salami sandwich in a lunchbox.

Individual pairs can devise further likely or unlikely conversations.

## Storytelling circle
You or one of the children say the first word of a story. Each child in turn adds a word and builds up the story.

As an extension, begin with a sentence, and have the children contribute a sentence at a time to make a more complex story.

Although this activity can be used for small group work, it's probably better to begin it with the whole group to make sure that everyone understands how it works.

## Sound machine
The children divide into groups and each group chooses an emotion for a machine. The first child gets the machine started by making a sound and a movement to go with it. One by one the others join in until all are working in the machine.

As an extension, choose a topic like shopping and have the children devise words or sentences, accompanied by appropriate movements, to add when it is their turn.

Once they have joined in, they continue to repeat the same words and movements. Each child should listen carefully to the words of the previous part of the machine, so that a story or scene can be built up. For example, 'I'd like that toy' could be followed by, 'No money, what a shame!' and then by, 'Oh yes, there's some in my pocket'.

When everyone in the group has joined in, the child who went first can stop the machine by gradually slowing down or by giving a prearranged signal.

**One-minute hot seats**
One child sits in a 'hot seat' and talks for one minute without pause or repetition on any topic that he or she chooses.

When the children have had some practice at this, you can make it more challenging for them by:
• choosing topics for them to talk on
• getting the speaker to draw a topic from a hat
• increasing the time limit.

**Can you hear me?**
In pairs, the children tell each other stories at the same time. While they are telling their stories, the children must try to listen to their partners' stories. At the end they tell back each other's stories as accurately as they can.

**Soapbox**
Divide the class into speakers and listeners. Individually, or in groups of two or three, the speakers decide on issues they feel strongly about. They then stand on their 'soapboxes' around the room and start haranguing the listeners about their particular issue. Each group or individual tries to attract as many listeners as possible to come and stand in front of their soapbox. After a while the speakers and listeners swap roles.

# *Drama and children with language difficulties*

Drama, through its use of movement, provides children with an effective means of expression which does not rely solely on verbal communication, and can therefore be of great help to children who are experiencing difficulties with language, or who are learning English as a second language. For, as we saw in the previous chapter, children can use movement to experience a wide range of concepts before they are able to verbalise them, and movement can be used to provide the link between concepts, or meanings, and the words that represent them. For instance, the position concepts of 'under, on top of, over, behind, between, beside, around, left and right' can all be explored through movement before the children are required to name them.

Drama is also a useful teaching strategy in an E.S.L. program because it deals with language structures in an everyday context, including the social and emotional problems that children go through in adjusting to a new country and language. Drama is valuable in learning language usage as well as in exploring and resolving problems that children may have.

At all levels, the dramatisation of stories, songs, playground games, poems and special festivals from the children's countries of origin shows others in the class the value of different cultures. National costumes, musical instruments and dances can be incorporated into the dramatisations. This enjoyment and appreciation of each other's cultures adds to each child's feelings of confidence and self-esteem. Information about the different cultures that contribute to your school can be obtained from the children, parents, community groups and from education systems.

Role play of real-life situations provides children with opportunities to practise language in different situations. Corners can be set up in the room where children with differing language abilities can play out situations: e.g., a home corner, a shop, the post office or a bank.

As children gain experience, these situations can be extended. Here are some examples.

'A fire has started in the kitchen—what should you do?'

'You want to get your money back on a faulty model aeroplane at the shop.'

'You want to send a present to a friend in Vietnam, but aren't sure which is the cheapest way to send it.'

'You want to close an account at the bank, but the teller is trying to convince you not to.'

Later still, the children can suggest situations that they would like to explore through drama. They can be suggested during class discussions or put into a 'class suggestion box'. The children who have made the suggestion can either take part in the role play or choose others to play it for them. Different solutions to the situation can be explored and in this way each child can decide on the best solution. Sharing problems with a supportive class can be extremely valuable for each individual.

# *Puppets*

Puppets can play a part in helping children who are reluctant to use language at all or who are self-conscious about speaking in a more formal or public context. Speaking through a puppet takes the pressure off the child, so that he or she feels more relaxed and speaks more freely. You will be surprised how effective puppets can be in transforming some hesitant talkers into quite confident speakers.

Most of the speaking activities outlined above could be performed through puppets. Indeed, puppets can be used to advantage in all your drama work. It is important, however, that the kind of puppets children use are appropriate to their manipulative abilities and their level of skill in drama. Puppets that the children make themselves will motivate them more effectively than bought ones, or ones inherited from another class.

Beginners and young children need puppets that are easy to manipulate. Finger and hand puppets with faces drawn onto the children's skin are quickly made and easy to use. Glove, sock, paper bag and junk puppets, made from cones, wool, fake fur, coloured paper offcuts and other scraps, can be incorporated into your craft program and used to enhance your language work.

You can quickly make a puppet theatre by stretching a sheet between two chairs, or cutting a hole out of a large box, or simply holding the puppets up from behind a low cupboard.

As children gain experience in handling simple puppets, they can move on to more complex ones. They can make cloth hand puppets by outlining the required shape (making sure it is large enough to fit over the hand), cutting out two of these shapes, sewing around the outside and gluing on the features. Papier-mâché puppets have papier-mâché heads and cloth bodies. The face can be built up by using wads of newspaper and then gluing strips of newspaper over the top. The head is then painted and the clothes fitted.

*Making and using puppets for performance leads to greater confidence in speaking.*

Shadow puppets are exciting to use with children who are ready for more challenging work. They are especially suitable for the stylised enactment of folk tales and legends, and as visual accompaniment to music that the children have composed. They can be made by cutting out shapes and taping wire onto the back (the wire serves as a manipulating rod). You can add colour by cutting out holes in the puppet body and gluing cellophane over the top. When light shines through the puppet, the puppet shape and the colours are projected onto the screen. A screen can consist simply of a piece of calico stretched over a wooden frame. Fold-out flaps keep it standing, perhaps on a table. A strong light, like that produced by a porta flood, is shone from behind the puppets and the shadows are projected onto the screen.

If you have a large screen, you can use the children as puppets to create whole-body shadow puppets. Children who are experienced in movement will enjoy being shadow puppets and will relish the experience of seeing their movements as they perform them.

# Drama and the reading program

In the previous chapter we looked at some of the ways in which movement activities can enhance children's enjoyment and understanding of the stories they read. Drama in all its forms is an excellent tool for exploring the ideas that children encounter in their reading, and is as good a way as any of motivating them to read more widely and with greater comprehension. Through role play children can explore and interpret characters and plots, problems and issues in a way that allows them to explore deeper levels of meaning. Reading a story or poem with a view to presenting it dramatically encourages them to read both carefully and imaginatively, and to try to understand not only what is plainly stated but also what is implied.

The following section suggests some ways in which drama activities can arise out of the children's reading, and indicates how these activities can benefit their language development.

## *Storytelling*

By telling stories in their own words children can practise and extend their vocabulary, and deepen their comprehension of what they have read or listened to. For beginners, the simple telling back of a known story is valuable. However, it's a good idea to provide a model by telling some stories yourself while the children listen and provide movements. Once they are familiar with this activity, they can take turns to be the storyteller while the others listen and add movements.

Story drama, as detailed in Ronald James' book *Infant Drama* (Nelson, London, 1967), is an excellent way of developing improvisation skills and preparing children for a book or a poem they are about to read. The following steps show how the procedures James suggests could be adapted to prepare a class for a reading of Pamela Allen's *Who Sank the Boat?*

- Tell the children the name of the story and discuss with them what it *might* be about.

- Select a number of actions that are described in the story: walking down the path; knitting a scarf; walking with an umbrella; jumping into a boat; falling into the water. Read the scenes that depict these actions while the children practise movement to show what is happening.

- Establish the setting for the story by designating parts of the classroom as locations in the story: 'Over there, next to the chalkboard, is Mr Peffer's place'; 'This line I am drawing on the floor can be the wharf'; 'That mat is the sea'.

- Divide the class into groups that represent characters in the story. So that everyone in the class will have a part to play, characters can be represented by four or five children. (This is particularly easy if the characters are animals.) Put the characters into position, describing how and where they should move: 'You five will be the cow; you will lead the others, starting over there at Mr Peffer's place'; 'This group will be the donkey; you follow the cow'.

- Then tell or read the story. Pace it so that each group has time to improvise its part. You can direct the children by pointing to areas they should be moving towards.

As the children enact more of these story dramas, they become accustomed to the way many stories are structured — the setting of the scene, a complication, the build-up of tension, the turning point and finally the resolution. This common plot structure provides a framework around which children will begin to build their own stories, both in drama and in writing.

Stories can be developed in class or group storytelling circles, where each child contributes a few words or a sentence when it comes to his or her turn. Though the story can well be based on a familiar original, you should encourage children to use their imaginations to provide interesting variations and invent new characters. In one class story circle Pamela Allen's *Bertie and the Bear* became *Silly Sally and the Bull*, and the children substituted new characters, actions and sound effects to replace those in the original story. The new story was recorded by the teacher, the children created their own illustrations and a puppet play was produced. It was a stimulating and rewarding exercise, in which the children gained valuable experience in exploring language structures through drama, and it showed into the bargain that they, like Pamela Allen, could tell good stories.

More experienced children will probably be ready to operate more independently by telling and acting out their stories in pairs or small groups. Different pairs or groups can try out different ways of telling stories, such as mime or puppet plays. An interesting experiment is to take a story that has been chosen by the whole class, divide the class into groups and have each group prepare its own version. Each group can choose the form in which it prefers to present its play to the class.

As an enjoyable activity for children who are experienced at devising and acting out their stories, call an assembly of 'the world's best storytellers' for a 'Tall Tales and True Festival'. Groups of children enter their tall or true tales (perhaps based on incidents that have happened to them) in the festival. The audience must try to pick the tall tales from the true ones. You can award prizes to the best guessers, or to the group whose performance fools the greatest number of people. Hold a party as the grand finale!

*The opportunity to enact a story gives greater understanding about its structure.*

# Reader's theatre

Reader's theatre is a form of scripted drama that relies for its effect on aural appeal and focuses an audience's attention firmly on a written text. There is a narrator who introduces and recounts the story, while others portray the characters. Very little or no costume or scenery is used, and movement is kept to a minimum; the action is conveyed almost entirely through words and other vocal effects. The narrator and the character players usually read from scripts.

When you introduce reader's theatre to your class it is important that you demonstrate the different roles, so that the children clearly understand the difference between the narrator's part and the other readers' parts. Until the class is familiar with the form, read the narrator's part yourself: later you can allot it to one or more of the children.

It is best to start with popular rhymes, chants and poems. With their strong rhythms and relatively simple ideas, inexperienced readers will find them easier to handle than passages of narrative prose. They also lend themselves readily to group presentation.

The following two examples of simple rhymes, taken from June Factor's collection, *Far Out, Brussel Sprout*, can be performed with considerable effect by children who are beginning to explore this form of drama.

> Mother, mother, I feel sick,
> Send for the doctor,
> Quick, quick, quick.
> In comes the doctor,
> In comes the nurse,
> In comes the lady
> With the alligator purse.
> 'It's the end,' says the doctor.
> 'It's the end,' says the nurse.
> 'It's the end,' says the lady
> With the alligator purse.

This verse is very simple to prepare as it already has definite parts for the narrator and the characters. You can perform it in small groups, or as a class with a number of children taking each part. Remember that the voice is all-important; everything depends on how it is read. Take time to experiment with different ways of presenting the text to create the best effect.

> Row, row, row your boat
> Gently down the stream,
> If you see a crocodile
> Don't forget to scream.

In this rhyme the narrator reads all of the text. The rest of the class is divided up into crocodiles and people in boats. The children decide what the crocodiles should say and what the people should say. Try it out until you are all happy with it.

Another very stylised but effective way of presenting this rhyme is for the narrator to read it first, and then for the people and crocodiles in turn to supply a slight variation — like this:

| | |
|---|---|
| *Crocodiles* | When you row your boat |
| | Gently down the stream, |
| | We crocodiles will frighten you |
| | And listen to you scream. |
| | |
| *People* | As we row our boat |
| | Gently down the stream, |
| | If we see a crocodile |
| | We won't forget to scream. |

In this sort of presentation, a group of children can play the narrator. When each group has read its version through, the group of narrators begins again and the others in turn join in to create a 'round'.

You can introduce longer poems and narrative prose as the children gain experience and expertise. Once again begin by working through the stories with your class to show them how to do it and to suggest effective means of presentation. The following guidelines should be helpful.

- Be thoroughly familiar with the story and make sure the children are too.
- Decide at the outset on the characters you will have in your version.
- If the story has to be shortened, make sure that the main ideas and characters are retained and that the story still flows well.
- Give all the narration to one child (or one group of children). The narrator links the different parts of the story and keeps it flowing. Changing narrators can disrupt the flow and is likely to confuse an audience.
- Help the children to experiment with their dialogue before writing it down in a final version.
- Make sure that every child has a written copy of the finished piece.
- Rehearse the text and encourage children to try out different ways of speaking their parts.

Eventually children will be able to adapt and write their own stories for reader's theatre. With practice, and by following the guidelines set out above, they will become adept at condensing longer stories into workable pieces. Children who particularly enjoy reader's theatre might adapt a long story into a series of episodes which they can perform at regular intervals to the class or in the library at lunch-times. Once children develop an enthusiasm for reader's theatre you'll find they come up with more and more ideas.

## *Improvisation*

In improvisation children make things up as they go along. They work without a set script or storyline. It is valuable in a reading program for the insights it can give into meanings that underlie a text. For instance, questions about what prompted a character to act in a certain way can be investigated by using improvisation.

For relatively inexperienced children interviews are a good way of exploring character motivation, and an example, based on 'Little Miss Muffet', will show how they can be used.

☐ Two children are chosen to be Little Miss Muffet and the spider. A chairperson introduces the characters, keeps order and chooses children to ask questions of Miss Muffet and the spider. By asking questions like: 'What were you doing before Miss Muffet came along?', 'Did you mean to frighten Miss Muffet?', 'Why did you sit next to Miss Muffet?', 'Did the spider try to eat your curds and whey?' the children investigate the reasons behind the characters' actions. At the end of the session the chairperson thanks the characters for coming and, perhaps, introduces the next ones.

Changing story endings is another valuable activity for children who have just begun drama. It gives them a feeling of control over what they read, builds up their confidence as writers and makes them aware of what goes on in a writer's mind when he or she writes a story.

For instance, one group of kindergarten children used their previous reading experience in an imaginative and creative way to change the ending of Pamela Allen's *Bertie and the Bear*. The children acted out the story and improvised a number of endings, discussing each one after trying it out and then suggesting a new one. They had also recently read Helen Nicol and Jan Pienkowski's *Owl at School* and been fascinated by Meg the witch. They hit on the idea of ending their story with a witch's spell, based on Meg's spell in *Owl at School*:

> Lardi dar lardi dair,
> Turn the bear into a chair!

This activity gave the children the opportunity to experiment with a new style of language encountered in their reading in which they had become interested.

While the children were improvising their drama the teacher took photographs that recorded various stages, including the endings. The photos were glued into a book and the teacher acted as scribe while the children suggested a text. The book was kept as a documentation of the processes the class went through in creating its new story and was used regularly as part of the reading program.

With some experience children can explore relationships between themes, ideas or characters through improvised role play. They can set up situations where at first characters from the same book or poem meet each other, and later characters from different books or poems. This requires the children to understand the characters whose roles they are taking. During the activity their roles are consolidated as they have to speak, move, react, answer and ask questions in role. You and the children can make up character and situation cards as a base for the improvisations. Examples might be:

- The crocodile from Roald Dahl's *The Enormous Crocodile* meets the dragon from Kenneth Grahame's *The Reluctant Dragon* to discuss what they find most pleasurable in life.
- Ginnie from Ted Greenwood's *Ginnie* meets Fieldsy from Lilith Norman's *My Simple Brother* in order to plan some adventures.

The more familiar children are with the characters whose identities they are assuming, the more convincing will be their improvisations. And, as they interact with others in role, they will become more keenly aware of the range of relationships that might exist between characters — from close friendship and affection through indifference to dire enmity.

Experienced children can be encouraged to look beyond the events of a story to explore external factors that might influence how the characters behave. These factors might be situations or people not mentioned in the story but which could have a bearing on it, as in the following example.

☐ Take a story like Doris Buchanan Smith's *A Taste of Blueberries*. Ask the children to suggest a number of people who do not appear in the story but might have influenced the narrator when he was coping with the death of his friend. The list could include a grandparent, a family friend and a teacher. Set up an inner circle of seats, in groups or with the whole class, where children take on the roles of these people and are questioned by the circle on their background and how they helped the young boy to cope with his loss. Divide the class into pairs and have each pair improvise a scene involving one of these people and the boy. Give the pairs time to review and refine their scenes before they show them to the class.

These improvisations can give rise to discussion about the importance of having caring people around you, the different ways in which people react to grief and the different needs people have in time of bereavement.

# Drama and writing

Whenever they are involved in drama, children are assimilating new experiences and exploring new ideas. Writing provides a natural outlet for these ideas and experiences.

Drama can give rise to many different forms of writing. Poems, stories, letters, diary entries, dialogue, and even scientific reports can flow from different drama experiences. At the same time, writing activities can be starting points for drama. Children often prefer to explore stories and drama scripts they have written themselves rather than the works of published authors.

## Writing as a stimulus for drama

Quite apart from the obvious stimulus that writing can provide for drama, writing can be used to help children build their belief in roles they are assuming. Documents, lists of belongings and written résumés of personal details all help to expand an imagined character and make him or her more credible. Activities that can help build a child's belief in a role include:

- putting together a folder of personal details about the character – name, age, sex, interests, occupation, dislikes, friends, special skills, etc.
- making personal documents for the character – driver's licence, passport, credit cards, bank books, bus pass, etc.
- drawing and labelling a map of hidden treasure that the character is searching for, or a map of an imaginary town that the character lives in
- making lists of supplies needed for a long trip the character is going on
- writing a brief account of a day in the character's life.

Children taking on roles of historical characters, such as Caroline Chisholm or Ned Kelly, may enjoy making written records of their research findings, or composing a short word portrait of the character.

## Drama as a stimulus for writing

At various points throughout this book we have suggested writing activities that could flow from particular drama work. Writing down improvised stories, recording dialogue, further developing in writing themes that were explored in movement — these are only a few of many examples. Indeed, there is almost no drama activity that cannot be extended in some kind of writing.

A drama resource box, in which objects like photos, pieces of jewellery, chocolate boxes, biscuit tins and driftwood are kept, is an asset in any classroom. The following activities show two ways in which objects from a resource box can be used to stimulate drama activities that lead in turn to writing.

☐ In this activity for drama beginners, an old chocolate box is passed around a circle and each child has a turn at feeling, looking at and smelling it. It is then passed around again and the children are asked to supply words — e.g., worn, pink and black, smooth, pretty — to describe it. The box is passed around a third time and the children think about someone who might have owned the box. One child is chosen to tell the others the sort of owner he or she thought of — e.g., an old man, a princess. The box is then passed around again, and as each child holds the box, he or she answers a question about the owner — for example:

- —What is the person's name?
- —Where does he/she live?
- —How did he/she get the box?
- —What sort of life is he/she having?
- —What are his/her hobbies and interests?
- —Does he/she have a family?

Gradually a picture is built up as important information and events in the person's life are improvised and decided upon. Then the children divide into pairs and each pair writes about one of these events.

☐ With more experienced children, you can follow a similar process by asking each of them to suggest a possible use for an object, such as a ruler, that is being passed around the circle. The children might suggest it could be a walking stick, a cricket bat, a magic wand or a conductor's baton. The next time around each child invents a name for the person who might have used the object, using voice and gestures to depict their character. The third time around the children, acting in role, provide some background for their characters — e.g., where they live and work, what they like to do. On large sheets of paper the children then draw their characters and write their stories. You can display the pictures and stories when they are finished. Children enjoy showing their work and it gives them the chance to read everyone else's stories and talk about them.

# 6 Drama for Performance in Years 3–6

Not all drama will lead to performance. Indeed most of the drama which you plan for your class will not be and ought not to be for showing to others. However, from time to time you and your class will be involved in a performance.

## The place of performance in a drama program

All too often performance is associated with the traumas and headaches of preparing for the inevitable assembly item, education-week display or end-of-year extravaganza. But performance should not be a one-off activity, with too much time spent motivating children and getting them to catch up on skills that should have been developed continuously throughout the year. To throw children into a large-scale production when they do not have the skills to cope with it is neither sound nor fair. Performance should be the culmination of a sequential drama program, bringing together the concepts and skills that the children have gained, and if this is the case, you'll find that not so many of those headaches occur.

Another problem with a one-off performance is the choice of extroverted children as 'stars'. If this happens every year, it may mean the same children being chosen each time. Many people remember their school performances as the times when they were the trees at the back of the stage, the toy blocks who were not supposed to move, or the person who opened the curtains. Of course such functions are all part of the staging of plays, but everyone should take turns in both cast and production crew. In a sequential program children can gain experience in many aspects of performance.

Performing drama created by themselves means a lot more to children than using scripts by other playwrights written in different times and places. Many of the activities discussed in this book could form the basis of a performance. Building a performance from that work means a natural progression is followed from first improvisations, through the recording, refining and polishing to the actual performance, which unites and celebrates all the skills, understandings and knowledge that the children have won in the process.

While beginners in drama are gaining confidence in the basic skills of voice and movement and are exploring the concepts of role and tension, it is best for them to perform within the class. After experience of these in-class performances, the children will be better able to perform for other classes. Performances for the whole school and for special occasions will be most valuable for children who have had a lot of experience in presenting their work to their own and other classes.

This progression from performance for each other, then for other classes, and finally for the whole school or for special occasions, is also a process that very experienced children should use in building up any work for performance.

## Performance within a class

Children's first experience of performing drama should always be within their own class, because it provides a non-threatening environment in which they can try out improvisations, movement sequences, puppet plays, reader's theatre and story dramatisations. Children get new ideas by observing each other, and by discussing their performances in the informal atmosphere of their own class, they can help each other analyse their work and find the most effective ways of getting their ideas across. Candid opinions about their work and practical suggestions for improving it can be got by asking their classmates questions like these:

- Did you understand what the performance was about?
- What parts did you understand best?
- Was there any part you didn't understand clearly?
- How could the performance be improved?
- Could you hear what we were saying?
- Did you know what character each of us was playing?
- Did our movements suit the characters?

Children can refine their work from the answers they receive, and you will find that they use suggestions in their future work too. Discussions like these are essential for developing quality in performance.

Within any class you are likely to have children working at different levels of experience. In preparing work for performance you may find that some children can be extended by being encouraged to help with direction or other aspects of production. Others might organise presentations to other classes or lunchtime performances in the library. It is stimulating for children at different levels of experience and ability to work together, and the more experienced can act as tutors and motivators to the others.

## Performance for other classes

Presenting drama to other classes involves sharing work with others who have not been involved in the same process of exploring and learning. It takes children away from the security and informality of their own classroom, and puts them in a more vulnerable and formal situation. Another class will expect to be entertained by a group of visitors and is likely to be more critical of shortcomings in a performance.

Before venturing into other classrooms the children should test their ideas on their own class and polish them into a work worthy of presentation. You should wait until children are thoroughly confident about performing in front of their classmates before you encourage them to perform for other classes. You and the children will know when they are ready to move out of the classroom.

# Performing for the whole school and for special occasions

As children take their performances to larger and less familiar audiences, the performing situation becomes more and more formal. In presenting their drama to the whole school, or perhaps outside the school on special occasions, children share their work with an audience that was not involved in the creative process and sees and evaluates only the end product. It can be a risky enterprise and only children who are experienced in performance should be exposed to it. Performing for a whole grade, and then for two or three grades, could be useful stepping stones on the way. Such performances can be treated as dress rehearsals, giving valuable feedback on aspects of the production. This scale of production also asks for serious consideration of costumes, make-up and sets.

# Choosing what to perform

There are many forms of drama available to your children for a performance; it's a matter of choosing one they are confident with. As far as possible the drama you choose to perform should reflect what you have been doing in classroom drama work and what the children are enjoying at that particular time. If they have been enjoying reader's theatre over a period, it's a good idea to build a performance from that. If they have been concentrating on movement skills and related concepts, they may decide to work up a dance sequence with music and costumes. A unit on body shadow puppets could culminate in a performance using a story they have enjoyed in their reading program. Improvisation work could lead to the children's making their own plays, recording them in a writing session and then developing them for performance.

Always try to let the children feel that they have made the decision about what to perform. By involving them in discussions about what they like doing and what is likely to be interesting to their audience, you will be able to guide them to make a good choice without making them think that it has been imposed from above.

# Organising a large-scale performance

Like any event that requires coordinated effort from a large number of people, a drama performance — whether it be for an assembly item, a Year 6 farewell or a play night during Education Week — needs careful organisation and planning. The following checklist should help you to establish priorities and to be aware of possible problems.

☐ Decide with the children what sort of performance they are going to do, drawing from the work they have done throughout the year. Will it be a play, for instance, or a number of items performed by different groups in the class?

☐ Find a suitable venue and make sure the production will fit into the school calendar.

☐ Make up a schedule that takes you up to the performance and includes target dates for completion of sets and costumes, rehearsals, etc. Look carefully at this schedule and satisfy yourself that it is realistic; being behind schedule is always dispiriting. It will also help you decide just what is possible in the time available, and you can tailor your performance accordingly.

☐ Organise resources, both human and physical. Are there any other teachers or parents (perhaps with special expertise to offer) who can help with aspects of the production, such as making sets or costumes with the children?

☐ Try to keep a record of the production process for future reference, using photographs, drawings, designs, diaries and videos (which will also provide pleasurable reminders for the children).

When preparing for a large production you will need a production crew. This allows every child to contribute to and feel part of the performance, and may also be a way of putting some of the available adult talent to good use. Consider some of the following:

- a director who helps the children to refine and polish their performances (this could be you, a parent, or a child with special skill in this area)
- a producer who organises the production teams (probably you)
- a costume team to design, make and look after the costumes
- a design team to design, make and look after the sets
- a props team to make or collect props
- a make-up team to collect and apply make-up
- a stage team to look after the curtain and the placing of the sets
- a sound team to devise suitable sound effects and provide music, of their own or others' making
- a lighting team to find out what lighting facilities are available and how to use them to best effect
- a publicity team to design posters, make tickets and organise articles in local community newspapers
- a front-of-house team to organise seating and collect tickets.

All these responsibilities are essential in a theatre and they should play their part in any larger-scale school production. Over a series of productions children can alternate between being in the cast and being part of the production crew, and the varied experience they gain will provide valuable insights into the working processes of the theatre.

## Costumes and sets

'Think simple' should be your motto when planning and preparing sets and costumes for a performance. A mood can often be more effectively created by simple means. A single green light and some eerie music will probably convey a feeling of mystery and intrigue more successfully than will more complex lighting and sound effects. A costume need only suggest the character, not the actual appearance of its wearer. Using basic props—such as long filmy scarves to suggest wind or an underwater world, or a wig and glasses to represent a mad professor—will usually work better than going to great lengths to achieve realism. Many time-saving devices can be thought up in the classroom by a discussion of what you want to show followed by a brainstorming session.

As a general rule, use your sets and costumes to provide the audience with enough clues to put them in the picture. Their imaginations can fill out the details.

A permanent and constantly growing collection of props is a great asset in the classroom. You will find that items like the following will often be used:

- assorted headwear — hats, crowns, wigs, etc.
- badges
- pipes
- walking sticks
- umbrellas
- glasses
- assorted items of clothing, especially those that can suggest the character or habits of the wearer — e.g., scarves, gloves, belts, ties, boots, etc.
- masks
- a telephone
- bags of various shapes and sizes
- large pieces of material.

Junk craft materials are useful for costumes, and so it's good to have on hand a plentiful supply of things like strong glue, wool, thread spools, tinsel and fake fur.

Scenes can often be suggested effectively by a few props; for instance, telephones on tables for a newspaper room, or large cardboard boxes for a hideout. If you decide to use painted sets, large sheets of cardboard, cloth or strong paper make good backdrops and are easy surfaces for the children to paint on. Children can experiment, too, with fluorescent paints and ultra-violet lights. As only the painted surfaces show when the light shines, these can be used to make skeletons and life-size puppets and to create a range of atmospheric effects.

## Make-up and masks

Children enjoy making up for a performance. You can build a make-up collection by asking parents for any surplus lipsticks, powders and puffs, rouge, eye shadows, liners and pencils. You will also need a large bottle of cleansing cream for removing the make-up. If make-up is to last, it needs to be stored properly: plastic tool boxes with separate compartments are ideal.

Masks can sometimes be more effective than make-up, and they are less messy and quicker to put on. With a supply of plaster bandages you and the children can build up a collection of sturdy masks.

To make a mask, smear a child's face with vaseline and mould the plaster bandages over the face — making sure to leave a breathing hole over the mouth or nostrils! When the bandages start to firm (after about five to ten minutes) ask the child to move parts of his or her face while pulling the mask off. You can use wads of newspaper covered with strips of bandage to construct facial features, and the mask can then be coloured with paint or shoe polish.

Less durable masks can easily and quickly be made from paper plates on sticks, paper bags, mesh orange bags or pantihose.

## Performers and their audience

In a performance the main aim is to capture and then keep the audience's attention. To help children communicate clearly and directly with their audience, make sure that they are aware of the following points as they develop and rehearse their items.

- Will the voices project to the whole space so that the audience can hear clearly?

- Do the voices use varieties of intonation, pitch and volume to reinforce the roles and make the characters more interesting?
- How can movement be used to portray emotions effectively?
- Do the performers look at the audience?
- Can the audience see the performers? In a puppet play, for example, are the puppets large enough to be seen from the back of the audience?
- Does the plot build up tension in a way that will hold the audience's attention?
- Are sound effects, music and lighting being used to create the right atmosphere?
- Do the costumes add to the performance by reflecting the nature of the characters or the feeling of the performance?

Children who are preparing for a performance must also be clear about what they want from their audience and the kind of reactions they can expect. They will understand this better if they have had a good many opportunities to watch other people perform. By learning to gauge the types of reactions—e.g., silence, laughter, verbal participation—which other performers are seeking, they will be better able to get these responses when they are performing themselves. Class discussion about different modes of audience behaviour will also help children to identify and understand them.

# 7 Drama across the Curriculum

Drama can be used as a teaching/learning strategy for a number of curriculum areas, including science, social studies, mass media and personal development. It can plunge a class into finding a solution to a survival problem for explorers or scientists, a planning problem for local government or environmentalists, a presentation problem for a news team, or a financial problem for a family. Because children are working actively in role, solutions to such problems are authentic and realistic. What they say and do carries greater meaning, as it reflects what they believe might happen in a real situation. Using drama as a teaching/learning strategy is often the quickest way to understand a concept, or see the details surrounding an issue, because the participants must grapple with all factors in their discussions and negotiations.

In this chapter we look at specific ways in which drama can be used to facilitate learning in science, media studies and personal development. When you have considered the strategies and techniques employed in these examples, you will be able to find ways of adapting and using them in other curriculum areas.

## Drama and Science
### 'Space Capsule'

This drama unit was planned for and worked with a Year 5 class (ten-year-olds) but could be adapted to suit older or younger children. The children in the Year 5 class had absolutely no experience in drama and had done very little group work of any kind. Their teacher had asked for a demonstration lesson to show how drama could be used in science, but had given no information about the previous work they had done. The teacher for this drama lesson, Anne Gately, had never met the class previously. The learning objective was determined from a study of the NSW Department of Education's Science K-6 Syllabus. The resources listed below are the ones actually used in the lesson, but they could be varied according to what you have on hand.

### Learning objective
To further the children's understanding of the process of forming hypotheses from factual evidence.

## Duration of the lesson
One hour.

## Resources
- map of the Milky Way
- map of the planetary system
- one pair of rubber snow boots (red with blue soles)
- diagram showing the internal systems of a simple computer
- a pair of fleecy lined gloves
- a large chiffon scarf (3m x 1.5m) with blue, purple and yellow spots on it
- butcher's paper
- textas
- blu tak
- a list of the children's names

## Teaching strategy
The lesson was based around the teacher in role as a government adviser. The class was asked to assume the roles of CSIRO staff who had been called to a secret meeting of national importance.

## The lesson
When the class entered the room, the teacher greeted them and introduced herself. (This part of the lesson was not carried out in role as the children had never met the teacher before. With a class familiar to the teacher, or in subsequent lessons, the roles could be assumed immediately.) The teacher then asked the class these questions:

*'Do you like doing science?'*
The response was fairly typical – most said 'yes' politely as most children will to a stranger; some spent the first minutes of the lesson absorbing the new situation and others were not much interested at all.

*'Do you like doing drama?'*
Again, the response was fairly typical – most said they didn't know; some nodded hard and others looked astonished.

Then the teacher told the class that she would like to work with them in a way that combined science and drama and asked for their co-operation in the venture. She pointed out that they would be scientists and would be working with the objects they could see in the centre of the room. (The objects mentioned in the resource list had been set out in the centre of the space.) The teacher explained the idea of role-playing and discussed with the class the kinds of work scientists do. One result of this early discussion was that the children's interest was caught by the prospect of a new and exciting experience.

The children were then welcomed to a secret meeting by the visiting teacher in role as a senior government adviser on foreign affairs. They were thanked as Australia's top CSIRO staff for giving up their valuable time to assist the government in this project. The roles of the scientists were developed further when the government adviser asked who in the group were computer scientists, who were astronomers, who were forensic scientists and who were general scientists. (This last category was added for those children who had not chosen any other role.) Clues were given to help the children choose their roles in this way:

'I understand we have some people here this afternoon who have been watching satellites and comets through large telescopes in the country. Could those astronomers put their hands up?'

'From my list, I see that we have quite a few people who know a lot about how computers work. Could those computer scientists identify themselves?'

'I believe that we have some experts in forensic science here, who can piece together clues about all sorts of mysteries from the evidence they collect and put through lots of tests. Who are the forensic scientists?'

This sort of questioning helped most of the class to choose a role — even if they chose a role because a friend did, and not because they particularly wanted to be that sort of scientist.

The whole group was then invited to examine the group of objects in the centre of the room. They did this quickly — in fact, they pounced on the objects but did so fairly quietly. When they had looked at and felt all of them, they were asked to sit down while the government adviser explained how the objects came to be in the room. The whole scenario was given a dramatic frame of reference so that they would have some idea how to proceed. This 'frame' was set by the government adviser as follows:

'Yesterday afternoon, these objects were found in a space capsule which was floating 50 kilometres off the coast directly east of here. [The school was in a coastal suburb of Sydney.] They were picked up by a naval patrol boat and returned to Sydney by helicopter. Because we have no space craft which could possibly have fallen into the sea, and because no people were found in the craft, we need some help with ideas about who put the space craft up and the reasons why it fell into the Pacific Ocean so near here. I have very little else I can offer to help you in your investigation, but if you are able to come up with ideas, this would greatly assist the Prime Minister. I'm very sorry that I can't offer you proper laboratory conditions and there's not much time, I'm afraid. I have to return to Canberra later today and can only let you examine these articles for an hour.'

By this time the children were totally absorbed in the situation and willing to assist in any way they could. The situation had become a real one to them and they were beginning to think as scientists. They were then asked to dispose themselves in their specialist groups of computer scientists, astronomers, forensic scientists and general scientists. One by one, each group was asked to send a representative to the centre of the room and collect the relevant evidence for that group to examine. About twenty minutes had elapsed at this point of the lesson.

The groups then settled down for the next twenty minutes with the articles of clothing, maps and diagrams, discussed them and recorded all the information they could on the butcher's paper. The government adviser answered any enquiries as well and as promptly as possible without forcing any 'plot' on the class. Questions such as, 'Were there any flags or symbols of a country on the space craft?' and, 'Was there a radio transmitter in the space craft?' could be answered quite openly with an 'I don't know, I'm afraid.' Such a response allowed the children to form the hypothesis that there must have been for a craft to be in the air at all.

After twenty minutes each group was invited to send a representative around to the other groups to find out whether someone had discovered something that might help another group's investigations. This took about ten minutes. It was now time to wind up the lesson and examine the hypotheses.

Each group selected someone to stand up and outline their findings, with the aid of the notes they had written on the butcher's paper. By the time all the evidence had been given to the whole class, the following scenario had emerged:

France and the United States were preparing to invade Australia because they were worried about the nuclear threat in Europe and because they felt that Australia would be safe from the USSR. Because they were traditionally allies of Australia, they had entered into this project secretly. The crew of the craft had been prepared for all sorts of emergencies of cold and heat but had probably drowned when the craft went down. It was imperative that the Prime Minister be informed of this threat of invasion immediately.

This hypothesis was developed from all sorts of evidence, some of which had been foreseen by the teacher and some of which had not. For example, the idea that France and the United States were allied against Australia was based on observation that the boots had been made in France — a fact their owner had never known before — and that the maps had been printed in the United States (the fine print on the back of the maps had been missed by the visiting teacher earlier).

The scientists were thanked by the government adviser, who was prepared to end the lesson there. However, one group of computer scientists came up with a brilliant idea — to send the Prime Minister a message by computer immediately, so that the government would know of the danger, and in case the return of the government adviser to Canberra was sabotaged. This idea was a natural extension from the scenario worked out, and could have led to a lesson on scientific writing.

### Evaluation

The visiting teacher was confident that the class had achieved the learning objective and that some unexpected outcomes were achieved too.

- The children were able to make decisions in a group.
- Many children had the opportunity to stand up in front of their peers and coherently put forward a reasoned argument.
- Boys and girls were able to work together in mixed groups.
- An opportunity for voicing their knowledge of and concern about world issues was provided.

The only concern the visiting teacher had was that the lesson would be a one-off for the class. The class teacher expressed her thanks but added, 'Of course, some of the boys might be real scientists but I'm not sure it was a good lesson for the girls.' In fact the boys had not shown any more or less expertise than the girls in their hypothesising, and the girls had been equally active in their examination, discussion and reporting. However, with more opportunity for combining science and drama, the class might have been able to change their teacher's mind.

## Role play in mass media studies

Role plays are a useful and enjoyable approach to mass media studies. They are especially valuable in helping children to understand concepts (such as construction of messages in the mass media), and to appreciate the processes of media production and the effect that messages and programming have on shaping their own attitudes and values.

Role plays for beginners should be structured so that the issues or problems are clearly understood by all participants. Children are better able to participate in more complex dramatic structures as they gain experience in drama. The following role play can be adapted to suit the general level of development and age range of any class from early primary school to junior secondary. The idea can be extended into much larger lesson units and the structures can be applied to different topics.

# 'The Ad Factory'

The main objective of this role play is to enable children to understand how their preferences and desires are often shaped by advertising, especially television advertising.

At the outset the teacher should outline to the class the structure of the role play by making these points.

- The classroom is going to become an office—this is the dramatic frame in which all action takes place.
- The class will not be students but expert artists and writers.
- The teacher is not an artist or a writer but the Office Manager. As such, he or she is able to help people with getting paper, pencils, paints or textas, but is not as good as they are at thinking up ideas for advertisements.
- The time scale of the role play is . . . (see 'Structuring time' below).
- The Office Manager is available at any time to help.

## The roles

In this role play, the teacher works in role as a helper to the class. Thus the role of Office Manager is appropriate as it enables the teacher to solve logistic problems, to supervise group work and to help children who are having difficulty working in role to make their roles more authentic. Roles the children might choose include:

- writer of songs
- writer of jingles
- writer of slogans
- writer of photo captions
- drawer of backgrounds
- drawer of human figures
- drawer of animals.

The children should work in groups. In each group the roles may be taken by different children, or they may all choose to have all of these skills.

## The first lesson

Begin the drama by setting the scene and announcing, as Office Manager, that this is the new office of an advertising agency called 'The Ad Factory'. The company has been very successful in creating advertisements which children like and understand. There are a lot of people who work for the company and some of them are new on the job. For that reason, you would like each person to tell everyone what speciality he or she has in writing, drawing or painting.

Some children may not be able to pinpoint a speciality at this early stage of the role play and, as the Office Manager, you can reassure them that they will certainly find their expert role as they spend longer in the company, and that you understand how difficult it is for people who are new on the job.

Tell the company that you have received a new product for which a manufacturer wishes to mount a television, magazine and newspaper advertising campaign.

Choose a product which might appeal to your class. Some suggestions are:

- invisible paints
- face paints
- computer games
- talking dolls
- items of clothing, such as jeans, shorts, T-shirts
- a summer fruit, such as watermelon or strawberry
- a common food, such as bread, milk, meat
- a bike safety helmet
- an ice-skating rink
- a waterproof sunscreen.

The manufacturer would like a 90-second television advertisement, a full-page colour magazine advertisement for popular monthly magazines and supplementary weekend magazines, and a half-page newspaper advertisement for local papers. Define what are the features that the manufacturer would like to emphasise. Some ideas may be:

- the cost of the product
- the safety of the product
- the glamour of the product
- the durability of the product
- the 'healthiness' of the product.

The main idea the manufacturer wants to come through in these advertisements is that the product appeals to children, as this will help to sell more of it.

Set up the workers in groups and ask them to prepare all three advertisements. Tell them that you will present their designs to the manufacturer when complete. The television advertisement has to be presented as a story-board and as a live presentation (this can be done as an improvisation for the rest of the class).

## Structuring time

At this point of the lesson, you will need to remind the class of the time scale within which you have chosen to structure the drama. You might allow between ten and fifteen minutes for discussion of ideas and then break the lesson to be continued the next day. This would enable the class to think about advertisements and to do some research. You might choose to go ahead and spend an integrated morning or afternoon working on the advertisements. The next day, another integrated morning or afternoon could be spent completing them for a presentation session on the third day.

The way you structure the time in this role play depends on your class, other timetable commitments and your own evaluation of the progress the class is making on the task. After your initial setting up of the role play, the class will be working in groups and your role will be that of assistant and provider of writing, painting and drawing implements. You might ask all the groups to work on their television advertisement in the same session, as children trying out movements, songs and jingles could disturb the concentration of others trying to create copy and illustrations for magazines and newspaper advertisements.

It's a good idea to ask a colleague (such as the principal or a teacher/librarian) to help in the presentation session. This person can assume the role of the manufacturer who chooses which advertising campaign he or she wishes to pursue — perhaps the newspaper advertisement of one group, the magazine advertisement of another and the television advertisement of a third.

# Drama and personal development

Drama activities can be valuable in developing self-esteem and cooperative and social skills, and in enhancing children's understanding of human relationships. They can also help to open up discussions about sensitive and difficult issues in personal development. Because children have the protection of a role, they are able to distance themselves from their words and actions by attributing them to a character. While they have to take responsibility for this character, they do not have to expose all their feelings and attitudes if they feel unable to do so.

# 'Our Place'

The following simulation can be used with children of different ages. It is most suitable for children who have some background in drama and some experience of group decision-making and group co-operation.

### Resources
- enough name tags and safety pins for the whole class
- up to 50 different-sized cardboard squares and rectangles, some yellow, some red, some green (they should measure at least 5 cm x 5 cm but no more than 15 cm x 25 cm)
- three large sheets of paper (1.5 m x .75 m)

### The roles
There are three families: the Ab family, the Uz family and the Op family. Divide the class into three groups of equal size as far as possible. If the number of children in the class does not divide evenly by three, one group will have to be slightly larger or smaller than the others. Each group represents the members of one of the families.

Prepare name tags for members of each family, making sure there is one for each child in the class. These name tags should suggest relationships within the families, e.g.:

- Ab grandmother
- Op second child
- Uz father
- Ab cousin
- Op aunt
- Uz eldest child.

Children select their name tags and pin them on. You can present the tags so that the roles are visible — which allows children to choose their own roles and join a friend's family if they wish — or you can place them face down like pieces in a game of Scrabble. This 'blind choice' method works well in classes with good social relationships; it gives the children experience in working and cooperating with others they may not know very well and helps them to develop skills in negotiating and compromising.

### A simple simulation
Set a time limit of between fifteen and twenty-five minutes for each family to design a house that will accommodate them all and provide for communal spaces which they all agree are necessary. Each family uses the coloured cardboard shapes to represent the rooms in their house.

When the decisions have been made and the plans laid out, the families visit each other in turn. They inspect each other's plans and listen to the reasons for the choices that have been made. For instance, one family might choose to have a large games room because a lot of people in the family like a variety of games, such as table tennis or computer games. Another family might have a lot of bedrooms and bathrooms because the people in that family like privacy.

As each family describes the house it has designed, the visitors can ask such questions as:

'Why didn't you put in a laundry?'
'How do these people get to the front door?'
'Do you think the kitchen is big enough for all the people in your family?'

This kind of discussion allows each of the families to gain insights into the interests, tastes and priorities of members of other families, and to see how these have been catered for in the decisions and compromises they have made.

## A more complex simulation

More experienced children can face the challenge of some complexity within the same structure. Depending on your learning objectives, you can add some complicating factors related to the design or location of the houses. Groups could, for example, be asked to resolve potentially contentious situations like these.

- One family has a smaller area than the others but can nominate one of its members to approach another family to bargain for a swap.

- From a number of specific and clearly described sites, each family must select a location for the house it has designed. (You can prepare the descriptions yourself or get the children to do it beforehand.) No two families can choose the same site. Make sure that some sites are more desirable than others by having, for example, a swimming pool or an established garden, by being on a corner, facing a beach or backing onto bushland.

  The families negotiate for the positions they want. To obtain the site with a swimming pool, a family might offer to allow members of another family to use the pool whenever they want to. To obtain a beachfront situation, a family might agree to swap houses with another family for a certain period each year.

  The compromises suggested and the deals struck will test the ingenuity of the children and enhance both their skills as negotiators and their understanding of the process of negotiation.

- There is no space for people over sixty and the families must decide what to do about their older members.

- Only two houses can have electricity and the families must decide how to allocate this service to everybody's satisfaction. Families may, of course, decide to break up their units and place all those who need heat or light for their survival or work in the houses with electricity.

The purpose behind this simulation is to develop the ability to compromise. Its basic structure could be applied to many other situations—the location of an airport, highway or shopping centre; the division of food, money or a natural resource like water; or the location of a neighbourhood facility, such as an oval.

Although simulation games are commercially available, your specific learning objectives will be better served if you can devise your own.

# 8  Two Case Studies

These case studies provide an insight into the way experienced teachers have programmed for drama. We hope that you read their experiences with interest and can find ideas to adapt for your own programs.

## Jill Charters—Kindergarten to Year 3

Jill has taught for eight years in schools in the Sydney metropolitan area and has experience as a drama curriculum consultant with the NSW Department of Education.

*Why do you teach drama in infants classrooms?*

In all areas of education, I have found that children learn by active participation — by doing. I believe that children gain greater understanding by being active participants in their own learning. By using drama as a teaching strategy, and by teaching drama as a separate entity in my program, I have seen children become more confident communicators. They develop greater facility in using more complex language structures and a broader vocabulary. Children who have considerable drama experience develop co-operative social skills more readily. They learn to take control of their own destiny and are excited by the opportunities presented to them for solving a wide variety of problems.

Drama lets children make their own decisions and become independent thinkers. This is important in the early years of school as we are trying to help children grow into responsible people. Each child is able to contribute to the group's total responsibilities by contributing his or her ideas to the drama. We value all the ideas of all the children. There is no right or wrong — no hierarchy of contributors.

*How do you organise the class when you teach drama?*

When I teach drama in these early years at school, I teach the class as a whole group. This allows children who are especially talented to initiate ideas and action and to stretch their imaginations. Those who are less confident or less able have these 'high flyers' as models and enjoy the stimulation of drama. The class finds models for language and action in its members — not only in me!

*How do you program for drama?*

I have two strands to my drama program. Firstly, I program for drama as a separate activity. In my Kindergarten class this year, we do drama on Monday afternoons. Secondly, I program for drama teaching strategies in other curriculum areas, such as language, social studies and natural science. This means that much of my program is integrated. For instance, music, health studies and drama can often be taking place simultaneously. With these two approaches, we do some drama every day. Many teachers I know have difficulty finding time for all the responsibilities we have in so many curriculum areas. That's why I think integration is the best approach to programming drama. I suppose, like most teachers, I tend to spend slightly more time on the things I enjoy teaching than on other areas of the curriculum.

*Do you develop your program alone or with colleagues?*

In my present school, I'm working with colleagues. This hasn't been the case in other schools where I've worked. At present, some less experienced teachers are very keen to learn about drama and I'm enjoying working with them to develop programs. Sometimes I act as a resource for other groups of teachers who would like to discuss teaching drama. I think I'll be doing more of this 'consultancy' work within the school as the year progresses. In other schools I've worked in, people seemed to be very busy just getting through daily workloads and travelling to and from school. This meant that less time could be spent working together on curriculum issues.

*How do you begin your year's program in drama?*

I began this year with an integrated movement and music program. We do these activities most days. We are doing quite a bit of story drama, with the whole class working together to explore one character in a story. Some time has been spent on smaller groups of children developing roles; we'll develop individual roles later in the year. Literature is a strong base for our drama. Sometimes we work on stories we know well and improvise changed endings. I think that this approach is a good way into improvisation for beginners, especially for Kindergarten.

We have also started doing some reader's theatre with nursery rhymes and songs. This is a wonderful form of performance for my class because they like sharing some special favourites with each other.

*What do you think drama has contributed to your development as a teacher?*

I think I teach in a more exciting classroom because I teach drama. The children are really turned on to drama. Stencils are a last resource in my teaching! I find the interaction with the children so stimulating. At the moment, I'm observing one child who obviously has great ability in drama. He seems to have a natural talent for understanding the development of tension and his work in role is really exciting. He's an exceptional reader and he initiates so many ideas for drama. As he's not quite five yet, I'm interested to see how his enthusiasm develops. It certainly ignites the rest of the class.

# Some examples of Jill's drama programming

## WEEKLY TIMETABLE

|  | Monday | Tuesday | Wednesday | Thursday | Friday |
|---|---|---|---|---|---|
| **09.00** | Movement | Movement | Library | Movement | Folk dancing |
| **09.30** | Language | Language | Language | Language | Language |
| **10.40** | Recess | Recess | Recess | Recess | Recess |
| **11.00** | Mathematics | Mathematics | Mathematics | Mathematics | Mathematics |
| **11.30** | Health | Italian | Natural science | Social studies | Natural science |
| **12.00** | Music | Singing | Singing |  | Music |
| **12.30** | Lunch | Lunch | Lunch | Lunch | Lunch |
| **01.30** | Drama | Art | Craft | Fitness groups | Creative activity groups |
| **02.15** |  | Play groups | Play groups | Play groups |  |
| **02.30** | End of school day | | | | |

Each language session includes literature-based reading, the writing process, speaking and listening activities and fine motor skill activities. All through the year I enhance my language program with the drama techniques of story drama, storytelling, puppetry, reader's theatre and improvisation.

I also use drama as a teaching strategy in my social studies, natural science, health studies and music programs.

I find play very important as a lead up to drama; that is why the children have play three times a week. The creative activities session on Friday afternoon gives children free choice of puppetry, play making, art, craft and music.

I program for three movement sessions a week in Term 1 because the children need to develop gross motor skills, body awareness and a repertoire of movements for their drama work. I integrate movement with music, health studies and dance. In Terms 2 and 3 I may cut down the movement times to twice a week, depending on the children's development.

The Monday afternoon drama time changes every four to five weeks. At the beginning of Term 1 the children work as a whole group on role. They rely on the teacher for many of their ideas. As they gain experience in working with the whole class and myself, they will be better able to initiate ideas, take on individual roles, build tension into their work and solve problems. The following grid shows the type of activities I would program to cater for their development over the year.

## DRAMA TERM BY TERM

|  | Term 1 | Term 2 | Term 3 |
|---|---|---|---|
| **Weeks 1-5** | Story drama: using fact and fantasy based on literature or made up by teacher | Improvisation: taking on group roles | Improvisation: taking on individual roles |
| **Weeks 6-10** | Reader's theatre: using known rhymes, chants and poems | Puppetry:<br>• dramatise stories<br>• make own play<br>• develop manipulation technique<br>• show other Kinders | Playbuilding: in groups from own ideas or teacher's |
| **Weeks 11-14** | Playbuilding: improvising with whole class on a topic | Masks:<br>• build<br>• dramatise stories<br>• develop own plays for the masks<br>• show them to other Kinders, then Years 1 and 2 | Preparation of their work for performance |

# Liz Davis—Years 4-6

Although presently working as a drama curriculum consultant for the NSW Department of Education, Liz Davis has taught in schools in the western metropolitan region of Sydney for eight years. She specialised in upper primary teaching at Bidwill Primary School.

*Why do you teach drama in primary classrooms?*

My education philosophy is based on teaching the child, not subject or curriculum areas. I look at the total development of individual children in my class—each person's academic, personal, emotional, social and physical development. I find that drama can be the focus for developing all these areas and that it's the most valuable teaching resource I have.

*How do you organise the class when you teach drama?*

My program involves small group and whole group work. This is how I think I can best meet all the individual needs in the class. To be practical, I set myself a list of priorities once I have planned my program. These include priorities for the total program as well as priorities for smaller units of time, such as a month, week, day or individual lesson. The rapport that is established between myself and the children is crucial for good classroom interaction, and that's the motivating factor in any classroom organisation I plan.

Name  Bernadette
Date  6th February 1986.

Name Something you feel you're good at   Netball.
Name one thing you need to improve   maths
Name one thing you'd really like to do that you can't do yet
be ateacher.
When do you feel happiest at school?  singing-

What makes you laugh?  When I get tichelled.
Name someone who makes you laugh  shane
What makes you angry?  when I get in truoble.
What makes you sad?  when someone dies.
What's the funniest thing that's ever happened to you?

What's the saddest thing that's ever happened to you? when I
broke my foot.
Tell about a problem you've had that worried you a bit
when I really fell down the stairs.

COMPLETE THESE SENTENCES
    I like myself when I Amnappy.
    I can't like myself when I'm angry.
    I feel happy when we are singing
I feel sad when I om very sick
I feel angry when when I intudde.
I am a person who likes to nicefriends.
I would describe myself as a nice          person
When I have a problem it's usually because I am angry.

When I have a problem I feel angry
I like it when pupils are allowed to dress up.
I don't like it when pupils arn't allowed to play.
I would describe myself as a good.          pupil
I like it when teachers are happy.
I don4 like it when teachers are not happy.
I like my friends because thay are nice.
When a teacher is angry it's usually because we mudi up
on her.
When a teacher is happy it's usually beause we are nice
to her.

*An example of a personal profile sheet.*

*How do you program for drama?*

I program all my drama work to enhance the self-esteem of the children in my class, and I base the program on their self-esteem needs. Each year, I begin with a self-esteem profile of the class. I get each child to fill out a personal profile sheet. Once I've had a close look at the information the children give me, I develop the drama program. Depending on the class, drama could lead us into movement and dance, into role play or into exploring some of the children's interests, such as mass media.

I frequently program thematic units. With a general theme like self-awareness, I might program different activities for different classes. Some titles I've used for these units include 'Being Us' and 'On Your Marks'. These titles are related to the information I found in the personal profiles. In units like these, lots of the drama activities are related to getting to know yourself and other people. As each unit uses an integrated approach to teaching and learning, we might paint self-portraits, paint designs based on our names, pose for individual photographs or write about the things we like, as well as undertaking drama activities. All the tangible products of the thematic approach are used to create a suitable classroom environment.

I plan an overall structure to my program for the year. Then I keep a day book, showing the activities and experiences we have. The program is continuously evaluated and one experience quite often becomes the basis for further planning.

*Do you develop your program alone or with colleagues?*

I've programmed both ways but have enjoyed working with colleagues best. At Bidwill, we worked as a planning group called a unit. My unit had seven classes in it from Year 3 to Year 6. After working together for a couple of years, we worked really well together as we had developed a great deal of respect for each other, even though there were philosophical differences in our approaches. At the school I've just left, I developed my program alone.

# A sample drama program

*This program concentrates on the drama strand of a language program and uses drama to enhance self-esteem and enrich language development. It is based on* Sadako and the Thousand Paper Cranes *by Eleanor Coerr (Hodder and Stoughton). Readers should note that Liz would not teach this unit as it stands but would integrate the aims and activities with other areas of language.*

## Rationale

The program was designed for a class of Year 5 children whose attitudes about themselves and their abilities suggested low self-esteem, poor social and inter-personal skills, lack of self-confidence and poor development in oral and written language.

The children had responded favourably to my reading of *Sadako and the Thousand Paper Cranes*. I decided to exploit this interest and use it as the content source for an introductory drama program which would explore feelings and promote collaborative learning.

## Aims

- To provide opportunities for the children to talk and move in fictional (make-believe) situations, as though the action were happening in the present tense.
- To develop the children's ability to work cooperatively with others and enjoy doing so.
- To develop the children's readiness to take on roles, interact in role and express feelings in role.
- To provide opportunities for the children to demonstrate an understanding of the main ideas and feelings expressed in the novel.

## Objectives

It was expected that each child would:
- follow verbal directions given by the teacher in the fictional situations
- speak and move as though a fictional situation, described to the class verbally, were happening in the present
- talk and/or write about feelings expressed in these fictional situations.

## Movement activities

☐ Run like Sadako. Stop. Lie down. Close your eyes and imagine how you would feel if you couldn't run anymore. Talk about it to a friend or partner.

☐ Run in slow motion. Imagine your legs are heavy. It is an effort to run. Freeze as if you were a photograph. Run really fast again. Stop. What differences did you notice? How did you feel?

☐ Stand in a space on your own. Pretend to be a crane flying. Use your space to fly high and then low. How do you feel? What can you see below you? Above you? As a follow-up, write about your observations in a poem.

☐ Find a partner. You are two cranes who meet. Move together as a pair. Stop and meet other pairs of cranes.

☐ Play a selection of Japanese music. Listen to the rhythm, volume and unusual sounds. In groups of four or five, create a crane dance to go with this music.

☐ Move around the room like a spider. Stop. Close your eyes and imagine you can see yourself as a spider. What do you look like? How do you use your legs and your body? Move around the room again
- searching for food
- running from a child who wants to catch you
- climbing your web.

Draw yourself as a spider after this activity.

☐ In groups of three, create a 'freeze-frame' of movement showing
- a crane
- a spider
- Sadako.

What does the rest of the class notice about each picture? Create a whole-class 'photograph' displaying different characters from the story. Repeat, swopping characters.

## Activities across the curriculum

- Make paper cranes and suspend them from the ceiling.
- Attach crane poems.

- Create a mural to display drawings, paintings, stories.
- Paint Japanese lanterns.
- Construct a giant spider out of plaster of paris.

## Language Activities

☐ With the whole class in a circle, each state one fact or main idea from the story. Then, in groups of four or five, select one of these (or a combination) to create an improvised scene from the story.

☐ In small groups, select a favourite part of story to dramatise.

☐ Improvise scenes beginning with:
'The most wonderful thing has happened . . .' (p. 20).
'As soon as we can afford it, I'll buy you a kimono . . .' (p. 25).
'Leukaemia! But that's impossible! . . .' (p. 27).
'I'm over halfway to one thousand cranes . . .' (p. 48).

☐ In groups of four or five, one child at a time assumes one of the following roles:
- Sadako
- Masahiro
- the spider
- a crane.

The others interview the character about his or her life, feelings, fears, hopes. Write a report on each interview as a record.

☐ In pairs, children take a role (as above) and have a conversation with each other. Tape record the conversation. Play back the series of conversations to the whole class and make comparisons. What do you notice about the characters? Which roles seemed the most convincing?

## Evaluation

The children's efforts in talking and moving in role were observed and assessed by the teacher according to the belief with which children approached their roles and behaved as though they were operating in the present tense. Though this was difficult for a few at first, my belief in their roles was crucial to their sustained belief. The discussions and writings about feelings, characters and events were records of the children's learning in role, and they reflected belief in role and understanding of feelings through direct experience with others.

# Reading List

Dawn Anderson. *I'm Four Potatoes: Drama for Schools*. Primary Education, Richmond, Vic., 1976.
Easy to follow, this book provides guidelines for the organisation and teaching of movement, relaxation and speech. Its many suggestions would assist the teacher beginning drama.

Curriculum Services Unit — Drama. *Drama is Primary*. Publications and Information Branch, Education Department of Victoria, Melbourne, 1982.
A very useful curriculum resource book, which covers all aspects of lesson planning, with featured chapters on ideas for the classroom and themes.

Eddie Errington. *A Time and a Place: Developing Improvised Drama in the Primary School*. Primary Education, Richmond, Vic., 1978.
A careful and well annotated approach to drama in Australian schools, taking developmental levels into account. Teachers are provided not only with a structured approach, but also a wealth of ideas for beginning drama and extended language and art activities.

Susan Holden. *Drama in Language Teaching*. Longman, Harlow, 1981.
This very useful book offers guidelines for language activities using drama, suitable for ESL and multicultural classrooms. A great many ideas and activities are given.

Sue Jennings. *Remedial Drama: A Handbook for Teachers and Therapists*. Pitman, London, 1973.
An excellent resource in practical style for all areas where special help is needed, including a multicultural emphasis as well as activities for physically, mentally and emotionally handicapped people.

Alan Maley and Alan Duff. *Drama Techniques in Language Learning*. Cambridge University Press, Cambridge, 1978.
This is an excellent basis and source book for teachers of ESL and multicultural classes. It provides guidelines for organisation, programming and evaluation, as well as basic activities.

Kathleen Manning and Ann Sharp. *Structuring Play in the Early Years at School*. Ward Lock Educational, London, 1977.
A wealth of ideas is offered, on a sound theoretical basis, for structuring young children's play and evaluating the results. Puppet plays, role play, simple playbuilding and imaginative play in costume are all related to the experiences of

the six hundred teachers involved in the project. Ideas are supported by detailed suggestions and related to the evaluation of educational outcomes.

Joan Miller. *Ideas for Drama*. Nelson (Springboards), Melbourne, 1977.
Any teacher interested in extending children's creativity will find this all-Australian production very relevant. Its extended units of work on six topics provide ideas for pair and group activities, and encourage discussion, social co-operation, and imagination. An excellent source of stimulus material including early Australian history.

Cecily O'Neill and Alan Lambert. *Drama Structures: A Practical Handbook for Teachers*. Hutchinson Educational, London, 1982.
An excellent source book for teachers of drama at all levels, offering approaches to drama, examples of lesson structures, teaching strategies and evaluative procedures.

Cecily O'Neill and others. *Drama Guidelines*. Heinemann Educational, London, 1977.
Seventeen lesson plans presented as case studies add a practical component to an attractive book for teachers. Drama in practice across the curriculum and aspects of drama including improvisation, role play and playbuilding are based on classroom experience from infants to junior secondary.

R-12 Drama Curriculum Committee. *R-12 Drama Curriculum Framework*. Education Department of South Australia Publications Branch, Adelaide, 1978.
A statement of principles for drama education, K-12, which provides a structure for the development of a drama curriculum. It covers the aims of drama education, a curriculum framework, features of programming and evaluation.

R-12 Drama Curriculum Committee. *Images of Life: A Handbook about Drama in Education, R-12*. Education Department of South Australia Publications Branch, Adelaide, 1981.
This book provides a basis for a drama program. As it is very detailed, it is useful for school-based curriculum development from pre-school to Year 12.

Ken Robinson (ed.). *Exploring Theatre and Education*. Heinemann Educational, London, 1980.
This fairly theoretical book, with value for experienced and interested educators, examines theatre and drama in schools, as well as the place of the arts, especially drama, in society.

Tom Stabler. *Drama in Primary Schools*. Macmillan Educational, London, 1978.
This excellent book is especially written for the primary teacher. It provides teaching strategies, evaluation guidelines and ideas for programming.

Betty Jane Wagner. *Dorothy Heathcote: Drama as a Learning Medium*. National Education Association, Washington, D.C., 1976.
This careful, practical analysis of the work of a major figure in drama teaching explains how to use drama to serve children, as well as to illuminate the curriculum for them.